Not Fade Away

Not Fade Away

The Life and Music of Buddy Holly

John Gribbin

ICON BOOKS

Published in the UK in 2009 by
Icon Books Ltd, The Old Dairy, Brook Road,
Thriplow, Cambridge SG8 7RG
email: info@iconbooks.co.uk
www.iconbooks.co.uk

Sold in the UK, Europe, South Africa and Asia by
Faber & Faber Ltd, 3 Queen Square, London WC1N 3AU
or their agents

Distributed in the UK, Europe, South Africa and Asia
by TBS Ltd, TBS Distribution Centre, Colchester Road,
Frating Green, Colchester CO7 7DW

This edition published in Australia in 2009 by
Allen & Unwin Pty Ltd, PO Box 8500,
83 Alexander Street, Crows Nest, NSW 2065

Distributed in Canada by Penguin Books Canada,
90 Eglinton Avenue East, Suite 700,
Toronto, Ontario M4P 2YE

ISBN: 978-184831-034-6

Typeset in 11 on 15½ pt Palatino by Wayzgoose

Printed and bound in the UK by
CPI Mackays, Chatham, ME5 8TD

Buddy Holly didn't give birth to
rock 'n' roll, but he sure rocked the cradle.

Carl Perkins

We used to watch *Sunday Night at the London Palladium* ... One night they had Buddy Holly on the show, and I thought I'd died and gone to heaven; that was when I saw my first Fender guitar. It was like seeing an instrument from outer space and I said to myself: 'That's the future – that's what I want' ... Of all the music heroes of the time, he was the most accessible, and he was the real thing. He wasn't a glamour puss, he had no act as such, he clearly was a real guitar player, and to top it all off he wore glasses. He was like one of us. It was amazing the effect his death had on us. After that, some say the music died. For me, it really seemed to burst open.

Eric Clapton, *The Autobiography* (Century, 2007)

For my friend in Lubbock, Texas – Bill Jolley

And for the next generation of Buddy Holly fans, Bella and William

Acknowledgements

Thanks to John Beecher for all of the Buddy Holly material he has supplied over the years, to Ben Gribbin for a critical reading of the first draft of this book, and to David Glasson for musical insights. Simon Forge and Michael Kenward played no direct part in the present project, but have shared many a Buddy Holly moment with me in the past five decades. Without any one of them, it would not have turned out the same way. Sonny Curtis and Kevin Montgomery took the trouble to put me right on some dates and other facts, Joe's Vintage Guitars helped with information about 1950s Fender Stratocasters, and Carl Bunch provided the playlist for the last tour. Gary and Ramona Tollett provided details of the 'That'll Be The Day' recording session, while Sherry Holley and Larry Holley helped with some family background. Quotes credited as (*Memories*) are from the superb collection gathered together by Jim Dawson and Spencer Leigh. The archive of the Buddy Holly Center in Lubbock is the source for the exact dates of his tours and other activities.

Special thanks to Warwick Bilton for technical help (see Chapter Five!).

For once, Mary Gribbin played no direct part in the writing of this book, but deserves thanks for tolerating my obsession with Buddy Holly for most of the past 50 years.

Although I have tried to check all the facts and make the story as accurate as possible, after half a century there is inevitably some uncertainty about the exact details of certain events; if anyone finds errors in my version of the story, or has additional information, I'd be glad to hear from them with a view to getting it right next time. I can be contacted via john@gribbin.co.uk

John Gribbin trained as an astrophysicist at Cambridge before becoming a full-time science writer, and he is the 'master of popular science writing', according to the *Sunday Times*. He has worked for *Nature* and the *New Scientist*, and has contributed to *The Times* and the *Independent*. His numerous books include *In Search of Schrödinger's Cat* and *Science: A History*. *Not Fade Away* is his first-ever non-science title.

Contents

Reminiscing

I wasn't quite a teenager when Buddy Holly died. On 3 February 1959 I was just six weeks short of my thirteenth birthday. The news of Holly's death in a plane crash, along with the Big Bopper and Ritchie Valens, made a relatively small impact on me at the time. It was the older boys at school who were shocked by the news, and stood in dazed groups in the playground discussing what seemed to them like the end of the world. I knew Buddy Holly and the Crickets from their hit singles played on the radio (Radio Luxembourg, listened to under the blankets in bed at night), but at that tender age I hadn't purchased any of them myself. My own musical taste leaned more to Lonnie Donegan, the Everly Brothers, Lord Rockingham's XI, and (of course) Elvis Presley. I was the proud possessor of the Kingston Trio's version of 'Tom Dooley' on a 78 rpm record.

But in the wake of the events of 3 February 1959,

the first 45 rpm record I bought was an EP by Holly containing the hits 'Peggy Sue' and 'Listen to Me', with their B-sides 'Everyday' and 'I'm Gonna Love You Too'. The first LP I bought was, curiously, *The Buddy Holly Story Volume Two* – so many of my friends had copies of the first *Buddy Holly Story* album, which was required listening at any gathering, that somehow I never got around to getting my own copy until years later. By 1962, I was enough of a Holly fan to be incensed when Tommy Roe had a big hit with 'Sheila', a blatant rip-off of 'Peggy Sue'. And my enthusiasm has remained at that level; nine of the top 25 most played tunes on my iPod are by Holly.

I'm in good company. The Beatles took the inspiration for their name largely from Holly's group, the Crickets; they took the inspiration for their early efforts at songwriting from Holly, and chose the Crickets' 'That'll Be The Day' for their first attempt at recording. George Harrison later said, 'Buddy Holly was my first favourite and my inspiration to go into the music business' (*Memories*). The Hollies took their name entirely from Buddy, while the Searchers took theirs from the name of the movie in which John Wayne repeatedly utters the line 'That'll be the day', itself the inspiration for the song. The

Rolling Stones first hit the UK top ten with 'Not Fade Away' – a Buddy Holly song. And Bruce Springsteen sings Buddy Holly songs in his dressing room to warm up before going on stage.

Without Holly, the British music boom of the 1960s, and all that it influenced, would have been very different. He was so influential because he could do everything – by the end of his short life he was not only writing the songs, and performing them in a self-contained unit with the Crickets, but was producing records too. Although the Crickets also performed as a trio, Holly's band essentially invented the now classic group line-up of two guitars, bass and drums. They sometimes dispensed with the second guitar, because Holly was also a superb and original guitarist who could produce a sound like lead and rhythm at the same time. Playing second guitar in Holly's band was about as pointless as the proverbial fifth wheel.

Elvis was undoubtedly a greater performer – but Elvis didn't write songs, didn't produce records, and was no more than a competent guitar strummer. Buddy Holly did it all, and he did it all so well. Appreciated much more in Britain than in his homeland, he was the inspiration for dozens of groups who thought 'If he can do it, so can we.' Some were right; many were wrong. But the ones who were right included the Beatles and the Rolling Stones. In the words of his biographer Philip Norman, 'there is a case for calling Buddy Holly the [twentieth] century's most influential musician'.

How did this phenomenon happen? How did a young man who was only 22 when he died, and whose career lasted just eighteen months from the time of his first hit record to his death, change the face of popular music? And why is he still so popular – the musical *Buddy* has now been running for nearly as long as Holly's entire life! The simple answer is, 'Because he was the best'. This book aims to look a little more deeply at the phenomenon, and explain how a Texan country boy from Lubbock became the best, travelling from country music to rock 'n' roll and beyond. The earliest known recording of Buddy Holly singing and playing the guitar reveals a frighteningly competent twelve-year-old musician – the same age that I was when Holly died. He was recording for at least ten of his 22 years.

It isn't my intention here to present a fully rounded biography of Buddy. Rather, I want to focus on the music that was the centrepiece of his life – both his own music and the influences that made him the musician he was, but especially his own recordings, rather than the minutiae of the almost non-stop grind of touring. None of us can go back to the Trocadero cinema in south London on 1 March 1958 to see and hear Buddy Holly live; but we can all play his recording of 'Rave On', and gain something by knowing how and when the record was made.

More literally than of any other recording artist, music was Buddy Holly's life. The story of Buddy Holly's life in music spans the ten years following that first recording; but the story of Buddy Holley (as he was born) begins twelve years earlier, on 7 September 1936.

CHAPTER ONE

Little Baby

Charles Hardin Holley was born in Lubbock, Texas, at 3:30pm on Monday, 7 September 1936. He wasn't actually such a little baby; family members say he weighed in at 6½ pounds. The local newspaper, the *Lubbock Avalanche-Journal*, reported him as a more hefty 8½ pounds; but they got at least one other important fact wrong in the birth announcement, which read in full:

> A daughter weighing 8½ pounds was born at 6:10 o'clock Monday afternoon at Clark-Key Clinic to Mr and Mrs Lawrence O. Holley of 7913 Sixth Street.

The baby was a late addition to the family of Lawrence Odell (or 'L.O.') Holley and his wife Ella, née Drake. They already had two older sons, Larry (born in 1925) and Travis (born in 1927), as well as a daughter, Patricia Lou (born in 1929). From the beginning of his life, Charles Hardin was known as Buddy, a common American nickname for the youngest boy in a family; the name even appears on official documents such as his driving licence. His surname, Holley, was shortened to Holly by a spelling mistake on his first recording contract, and Buddy kept it as his professional name; the mis-spelling was common (L.O.'s name is written as 'Holly' on Buddy's birth certificate), and he probably felt that he might as well go with the flow. For consistency, I'll always refer to him as Buddy Holly.

Lubbock is a city on the dry plains of northern Texas, far away from the bright lights of places like Houston and San Antonio, and named after a Texan hero of the Civil War, Thomas S. Lubbock. In the United States, the term 'city' doesn't have quite the same connotations that it has in Europe – it simply refers to an urban area with some degree of self-government, for example, with an elected mayor. Some US cities have populations of under a thousand people, while others are measured in hundreds of thousands. Lubbock lies 300 miles west of Dallas and 124 miles south of Amarillo on Interstate 27. It was founded in 1891, less than 50 years before the birth of Buddy Holly, as a centre of the cotton-farming industry, and the population only reached 4,000 in 1920, although it soared to more than 20,000 over the next ten years. By 1930, the city's history proudly recalls, it also had three banks.

Texas itself didn't join the Union until 1845, nine years after gaining its independence from Mexico, so in spite of its latitude it has a distinctly different history from that of the old southern states of Alabama, Georgia, Louisiana, Mississippi and South Carolina. Apart from cotton, the only other important activity in Lubbock is the university, founded in 1923 as Texas Technical College and now known as Texas Tech, today offering 150 degree courses and with more than 28,000 enrolled students.

Lubbock is in the Bible Belt of America, claiming to have more churches per head of population than any other city in America. Right up until 1972 it was officially alcohol-free, and for almost as long it was racially segregated. Texas isn't always regarded as part of the formerly segregated 'Deep South' by non-Americans, but to put this in perspective, Lubbock is actually at about the same latitude as the heart of the state of Georgia, birthplace of Little Richard.

So Buddy Holly grew up in a poor but hard-working and loving family, in an out-of-the-way corner of America where religion played a big part in everyday life, but where black people and Hispanics were regarded as racial inferiors. One result of this was that he had little contact with blacks until he discovered their music. He was born in the midst of the Depression, when his father had to take a succession of low-paid jobs to support the family, and they had to move house half-a-dozen times in twelve years in the constant search for affordable accommodation. The house where he was born, at 1911 6th Street, was a simple single-storey building no bigger than a modern holiday chalet; the site is now an empty lot. But Lubbock doesn't seem to have suffered as severely from the Depression as many parts of the country – L.O. always seems to have been able to find work of some sort.

On his mother's side, Buddy could claim some exotic ancestry. Her grandmother was a full-blooded Cherokee, and Larry Holley recalls his half-Indian grandfather's pride in his native American ancestry. That made Buddy one-eighth Cherokee. Somewhat less romantically, Ella Drake's family belief that they were descended from the famous privateer Sir Francis Drake cannot be true, since the Elizabethan adventurer had no children. She had married L.O. in 1924, and was 34 when Buddy was born; L.O. was a year older than her. He had been raised on a farm near the town of Honey Grove, less than 100 miles from Dallas and even closer to Paris, Texas, but moved to Vernon, Texas, some 150 miles to the east of Lubbock, to find work. He also found Ella Pauline Drake there, but they moved to Lubbock a year after their marriage because there were better prospects of work in an expanding city, where Ella's parents had migrated a little earlier. The Holleys belonged to the Tabernacle Baptist Church, one of many splinter groups in the American South, which teaches an almost literal interpretation of the Bible and expects a tithe of (usually) 10 per cent of the earnings of its followers.

All of this may give the impression of a grim Depression childhood for Buddy; but such an impression would be wrong. He was the indulged youngest child of the family, doted on by his mother and with two big brothers that he hero-worshipped. He certainly had an easier life than his siblings, and was the first member of the family to graduate from high school. Although lacking other forms of entertainment, the family were all (except L.O.) musical. Larry played violin and piano, Travis accordion and later guitar, and Ella and Pat could sing.

The two older brothers performed together at local talent shows, with Buddy eager to join in. When he was five, his parents bought him a toy violin and prevailed upon Larry and Travis to let him 'accompany' them at one of these competitions. Since Buddy couldn't actually play the instrument, Larry smeared the strings with grease so that it wouldn't make a sound; but the judges were so taken with the cute kid sawing away and singing alongside his big brothers that they won a $5 prize.

Larry in particular became a role model for Buddy – a hard-working, adventurous character, afraid of nothing. Buddy, says Larry, was 'a cute little kid' who enjoyed being pulled around the yard in an old apple crate, as if he were on a sled; 'he really liked that.' But not long after Buddy's success in the talent show, the Japanese attack on Pearl Harbor brought America into the Second World War, and both Larry and Travis eventually left to join the Marines. Both survived to return home. Travis, who fought at Iwo Jima in February 1945, brought with him a guitar, bought from a shipmate, which he taught Buddy to play. Larry was among the soldiers earmarked for the invasion of the main island of Japan, and his life was among those almost certainly saved by the use of the atomic bombs that forced the Japanese surrender; the High Command had anticipated 90 per cent casualties in the invasion.

Buddy's interest in music had stagnated somewhat after that talent show, and although he began taking piano lessons at the age of eleven, after nine months he decided that this wasn't what he wanted to play, even though his teacher had told his parents that he was a quick learner and one of her best pupils. He dropped the piano and decided to switch to the guitar after listening to one of his fellow pupils on the school bus playing and singing on the daily journey, and his parents, ever-indulgent, bought him a steel guitar. That didn't suit him either, and he asked for one like his brother had; it duly came, from a pawnshop. Travis taught him the basics, but before long Buddy, who had a musical ear and learned to play by listening, not by reading music, was telling Travis where he was going wrong. 'He was a quick study and learned fast. In fact, before long he was showing *me* new things … He'd say, "There's another chord that goes in there, Trav."' (VH1) From then on, the family recall, Buddy was hardly ever seen without a guitar in his hands. He would play on the school bus with his friends, at home in his room, and sitting out on the front steps. The music he played was, of course, country and western, *the* big sound of the 1940s in the American South.

American country music had its origins, musically speaking, in an amalgamation of traditional styles brought to the New World by settlers; but instead of sticking to the traditional subject of love, the lyrics tended to deal also with practical events in the everyday working life of people like ranchers ('cowboy' or 'western' songs) and miners, and with disasters and tragedies such as train wrecks and murders. By the mid-1920s, 'hillbilly' music was being both recorded and broadcast on the radio; a good example is Harry McClintock's 'Big Rock Candy Mountain' from 1928. The first real stars of the genre were the Carter Family, a vocal trio who wrote literally hundreds of songs in the 1920s and 1930s; one member of the original trio, Maybelle, was the mother of June Carter, who wrote 'Ring of Fire' and married Johnny Cash. Other influential artists of the time were Jimmie Rodgers and Gene Autry.

Where Buddy grew up, though, the important part of the name 'country and western' was 'western', which essentially refers to West Texas. It stemmed from a marriage between country music and big-band jazz, developed in the 1930s, originally in a band featuring vocalist Milton Brown and fiddler Bob Wills. Wills went on to form the Texas Playboys, producing a string of hits in the late 1930s and 1940s, including 'New San Antonio Rose' in 1940. The western brand of C&W was very much music to dance to, at hops, jamborees and hoe-downs, which led to a more experimental approach to the music and the early acceptance of instruments such as electric guitars and drums – drums in particular were anathema in the traditional country music of the old states of the South, such as Tennessee, the home of the country music capital, Nashville. The other important feature of western music was that everybody played it – or at least, everybody played some kind of music, except for the few, like L.O. Holley, who couldn't carry a tune. This must have originally been because there was nothing else to do for entertainment in West Texas, but the tradition of playing in bands not just at school but among groups of friends, performing for each other and anyone else who would listen, was firmly established by the time Buddy Holly began to take a serious interest in music in the 1940s. So there was nothing unusual about Buddy's musical activity and aspirations; in that sense, he was very much a product of the time and place where he was born. It's just that he was so much better than all the other kids who picked guitar for a hobby and dreamed of becoming a star.

One of those other kids was Buddy's friend, Bob Montgomery, who featured strongly in Buddy's musical development in the 1950s; but they didn't meet until 1949. Buddy's first school had been the Roscoe Wilson Elementary School, in the city of Lubbock proper; but in 1946 the need to find cheaper accommodation forced the Holley family to move outside the city limits. Buddy had to transfer to the Roosevelt Elementary School, which involved the long bus ride on which he first heard a fellow pupil playing the guitar, and where he later played his own guitar and sang songs, including Bill Monroe's 'Gotta Travel On', to entertain the other students. At the age of twelve, partly thanks to his musical prowess, Buddy was the most popular boy in his class, recognised when he was voted, together with a girl named Barbara Denning, 'King and Queen of the Sixth Grade'. It was around this time, in 1949, that Buddy recorded himself performing Hank Snow's 'My Two Timin' Woman' (bizarrely inappropriate material for a twelve-year-old!) on a wire recorder that a friend who worked in an electronics store had 'borrowed'. There must have been other recordings made at the time, but none seem to have survived; this 1½-minute song is all we have from the pre-teenage Buddy.

Apart from the quality of the performance itself, the most important thing about the recording is that it highlights the kind of music that Buddy was listening to on the radio and being influenced by. Snow was a Nashville-based country music star, best remembered now for his 1950 hit 'I'm Movin' On'. Musically, 1949 was also an important year not just for country music but for pop music in general, with the emergence of Hank Williams, already a major country star, as a mainstream 'crossover' artist, with the huge success of his definitive recording of 'Lovesick Blues'. Williams' music could be heard in Lubbock thanks to his live broadcasts on country music stations – the *Louisiana Hayride* on KWKH from Shreveport, throughout 1948, and the *Grand Ole Opry* on WSM from Nashville, where he started in 1949. Buddy was fascinated by the Hank Williams sound, which involved a semi-yodelling style that stretched and bent individual syllables of words over several notes, and tried to copy it. But as John Goldrosen has pointed out, there was more to it than that. Williams wrote songs from the heart, drawing on his personal life and speaking directly to his audience, rather than simply performing (in effect, acting) someone else's message. The fact that so many of his songs dealt in a plaintive or wistful fashion with lost or unrequited love simply made them even more appealing to teenagers (and precocious sub-teenagers).

17

Another big influence on both Buddy Holly and Bob Montgomery was the brand of country music known as bluegrass. Bluegrass is based on acoustic stringed instruments, in particular the fiddle, banjo, guitar, mandolin and stand-up bass. The term originated with the band Bill Monroe and his Bluegrass Boys, which had this classic line-up, although other instruments, such as the accordion, are also sometimes featured. It was his interest in bluegrass music that explains why Buddy took up the banjo in the late 1940s and even taught himself to play the mandolin, although the guitar remained his main instrument. There are similarities between bluegrass music and jazz, because in each case the instruments take turns playing the melody and improvising on it, while the others provide the backing. This can lead to exciting 'duelling' between the instruments; fascinating, and challenging, to any competent budding musician.

Monroe formed his band in 1939, but developed the definitive bluegrass style between 1946, when banjo player Earl Scruggs joined the line-up, and 1948, soon being copied by others. This line-up of the band also featured singer-guitarist Lester Flatt; Flatt and Scruggs left the Bluegrass Boys in 1948 to form their own equally influential group, the Foggy Mountain Boys. Much later, Scruggs recorded with saxophonist King Curtis, who also played on Buddy Holly's record 'Reminiscing'.

Another influence on Buddy Holly came from country duet performers, close harmony teams such as the archetypal Louvin Brothers (real brothers, but originally named Ira and Charlie Loudermilk; the singer-songwriter John D. Loudermilk, who wrote Eddie Cochran's 'Sittin' in the Balcony', is their cousin). In the late 1950s, this style was developed in pop by the Everly Brothers, and through them influenced such artists as the Beach Boys and the Beatles.

Not long after Buddy recorded 'My Two Timin' Woman', an upturn in the family's fortunes enabled them to move back into the city of Lubbock, where they lived at 3315 36th Street. This meant that at the age of thirteen Buddy started seventh grade at the J. T. Hutchinson Junior High School, where he was reacquainted with some of his peers from Roscoe Wilson Elementary, and made new friends as well. Among his circle of acquaintances were Bob Montgomery, Don Guess, and Jerry Ivan 'J.I.' Allison, who was actually a grade below Buddy in school. Montgomery could sing and play guitar; Guess played steel guitar and stand-up bass, and was already writing songs; Allison played the drums. But at first, they didn't all play together.

It was Buddy and Bob who first started to make their own music as a team, developing a mixture influenced by both bluegrass and rhythm 'n' blues, which they heard on the radio from a show called 'Stan's Record Review', broadcast every night at 10:30 by KWKH in Shreveport, Louisiana. R&B was at the time entirely black, or 'race', music, and it was not considered respectable for decent, white Baptist boys to even listen to it, let alone play it.

It's widely accepted that R&B originated in the late 1930s and early 1940s, linked to the rise of radio and television and the availability of tape recorders, which made it possible for independent record producers to both make records and get them heard. The single most important originator of the music was Louis Jordan, a former jazz musician, who started recording with a small group in 1938 in a style known as jump blues. This rapidly spread, developing regional variations, around cities such as New Orleans, Louisiana, and Memphis, Tennessee. Jordan's influence can be directly traced through later artists such as Chuck Berry, B.B. King and James Brown, with Chuck Berry and Little Richard in particular developing it into rock 'n' roll.

The lyrics of early R&B were often not so much suggestive as explicitly sexual, and the term 'rock 'n' roll' itself came originally from R&B as a euphemism for sex, as is clear in Roy Brown's classic 'Good Rocking Tonight', a hit for Wynonie Harris in 1948, which Holly himself later recorded, as did Elvis Presley. The sexual connotations were an attraction for the teenage duo, but the music was what really mattered, and it was the quality of the R&B performances put on record by black musicians that led Holly to revise the racially prejudiced attitudes he had grown up with. Unlike many of the white kids, who found the softer sound of black groups like the Drifters or the Clovers appealing, Buddy and Bob became fans of the real blues and superior musicianship offered by artists such as Lightnin' Hopkins, Muddy Waters, Howlin' Wolf and Little Walter.

The appeal of such music was enhanced for white teenage boys by its flavour of forbidden fruit. Parents frowned upon it, and even those radio stations that broadcast it from distant locations like Louisiana mostly aired it late at night. As they grew older, Buddy and his friends would listen in one of their (or their parents') cars, straining to catch the sounds as the signal faded in and out, turning the car around when the music faded, to try to get better reception.

Although still strictly amateurs, as well as practising together and listening to music, Buddy Holly and Bob Montgomery seized any chance they could to perform in front of an audience, and quickly built up a reputation at school. In 1950, they were asked to perform a number as part of the entertainment for a parents' night at J. T. Hutchinson Junior High, but the organisers of the event didn't bother to ask them what song they were planning to sing. The staid adult members of the audience were shocked when the two teenagers chose to perform the song 'Too Old to Cut the Mustard', which they dedicated, tongue in cheek, to their teachers. A Bill Carlisle song, it recounts how when the singer was young he had to 'fight the girls off with a stick', but that now they say he makes them sick, because he's 'too old to cut the mustard'.

It seems a harmless enough bit of schoolboy fun today, but in 1950 Bible Belt America it was so outrageous that the embarrassed Ella Holley was seriously worried that her son would get expelled from school for his cheek. Wisely, though, the teachers ignored the incident. The students, however, were impressed both by the duo's nerve and by their performance itself. It was this show that first made Jerry Allison aware of Buddy Holly's talent, although the two of them didn't get together until they were in high school proper a couple of years later.

The move to the Thomas S. Lubbock High School, known locally as 'LHS', happened for Buddy and Bob in 1952, when Buddy was sixteen. The same year, they made home recordings of two songs which have survived as scratchy acetates, the quite listenable 'I'll Just Pretend', with Bob singing lead while Buddy plays mandolin and sings harmony, and the badly damaged 'Take These Shackles From My Heart', with Buddy taking the lead vocal. A year or so later they recorded the Bill Monroe song 'Footprints in the Snow' under similar circumstances, again with Montgomery taking the lead vocal. These home recordings, and the move to LHS, effectively mark the end of Buddy Holly's musical babyhood. By 1953, he was already performing on a professional basis as one half of a duo – though not with Bob Montgomery – and they were about to make their (unpaid) debut on a local radio station, KDAV.

CHAPTER TWO

Learning the Game

In 1951, the year Buddy turned fifteen and started his final year at junior high, two things happened to change his life. The first seemed trivial, or at worst an inconvenience. The school nurse noticed that he had poor eyesight, and an optometrist's examination showed that his uncorrected vision was only 20/800 in both eyes. A person with 20/40 vision can only see from 20 feet what a person with normal vision can see from 40 feet, so Buddy could only see from 20 feet what a person with normal vision can see from 800 feet. Some accounts say that he was 'legally blind', since 20/200 vision or worse is considered legally blind in the US – but only if that is the *corrected* vision. With glasses, Buddy could see OK, so he certainly wasn't legally blind (if he had been, he couldn't have had a driving licence). Like many adolescents, though, he was embarrassed by the nerdy look that glasses gave him, and he chose inconspicuous frames which he avoided wearing whenever possible.

This was more of an inconvenience for Buddy than for most of his short-sighted peers, because around the same time he started performing music on a slightly less amateur basis. It started when L.O. Holley was working on a building site where a young carpenter's assistant, Jack Neal, used to entertain the crew by singing and playing his guitar during lunch breaks. Neal, who had been born in Fort Worth, Texas, on 3 March 1934, was an accomplished musician and a big fan of country singers such as Hank Williams and Ray Price, who took over Hank Williams' band, the Drifting Cowboys, when Williams died. (In 1954 Price wrote 'Release Me', later a huge hit for Englebert Humperdinck.) After hearing Neal play, L.O. suggested that he should get together with Buddy, and they soon became firm friends and dedicated practice partners. A rugged, outdoors type (in spite of his slight stature), Neal also took Buddy, two years his junior, out hunting and fishing. But music was the core of their relationship, with Jack playing rhythm and doing most of the singing while Buddy played lead. They played every gig they could get, including entertaining the kids at local movie theatres before the Saturday morning shows; it was the audience response they got in such unpromising surroundings that encouraged Buddy to begin to think seriously about making a career in music. Early in 1953, in an essay written for a school assignment, he wrote: 'I have thought of making a career out of western music if I am good enough.'

Around the same time, Niki Sullivan, another student at LHS but a year younger than Buddy, saw Holly performing knock-out versions of Hank Thompson's 'Wild Side of Life' and Lloyd Price's 'Lawdy, Miss Clawdy' (both released in 1952) in school one lunchtime. Even though he was just sixteen, the choice of songs encapsulates the way Holly would change popular music – one a country classic, very much white man's music, the other all-out R&B, or race music. As much as anyone, it was Holly who put the two together to make rock 'n' roll.

Music was by far the most important thing in Buddy Holly's life even at this early stage. Sullivan, who later became one of the Crickets, was reported as saying that if Buddy had a choice between playing his guitar and going on a date, he'd play his guitar wherever there was an audience. But, like other red-blooded American teenage boys of his time, he was also interested in girls, drink, and smoking.

Although Lubbock was officially dry, it was easy to get hold of beer, which was just about all Holly could handle because of a stomach problem, later diagnosed as an ulcer. This didn't stop him occasionally drinking to excess, but the dire consequences (and parental disapproval) meant that this happened only rarely. Smoking was also something his parents disapproved of, and which he tried unsuccessfully to hide from them; but in the fifties this was not only widely socially acceptable but almost a required symbol of male maturity. Experimenting with sex, as most teenagers do, Buddy also dated several of the 'wrong sort' of girls as far as his parents were concerned; but the one he settled on as his steady date went so far in the other direction that in the end it led to the break-up of their relationship.

Buddy had met Echo McGuire when they were both children at the Roscoe Wilson Elementary School. They were in the same grade – their birthdays were just four months apart – and they had both been delivered by the same doctor, but in different hospitals. Although they lost touch when the Holleys temporarily moved out of the city, they were in the same circle of friends at junior high and then at LHS, and Buddy and Bob Montgomery used to play table tennis with Echo at the McGuire house. Echo's family were considerably more affluent than the Holleys; her father owned a dry-cleaning business, as well as his own house in a nice part of town, while the Holleys lived in more modest rented accommodation. They also attended a different church, which meant far more in 1950s America than it would in England today.

The McGuires were members of the Church of Christ, a sect so strict that it regarded music as the work of the devil, and forbade it even in church; girls who shaved their legs were regarded as fallen women, and dancing was strictly not on the agenda. It's hard to think of anyone less suited, on those grounds, for Buddy Holly. But Echo was an attractive doll of a girl, just five feet tall, her face framed in a halo of dark hair. She was also intelligent – a 'straight A' student – but deeply committed to her religion, and even at that early age planning a career in the ministry. Nevertheless, in 1952, in the autumn of their first year at LHS, Buddy asked Echo for a date, and she accepted. They went to a football game together, then on to the Hi-D-Ho drive-in, a favourite fast-food establishment where teenagers could cruise around checking out who was there (and who they were with) before pulling up for a burger or one of the 'Hidey' specials. The situation was slightly awkward because Bob Montgomery also wanted to date Echo; but in any case her mother said she was too young to go steady, so for a time she would go out with one of them on a Friday and the other on the Saturday. But by the spring of 1953 she had stopped dating Montgomery and was going steady with Buddy, who had won over her parents with his charm.

Although Buddy didn't even kiss Echo until they had been dating for a year, the relationship was a serious one which lasted through high school and ended only after Echo had gone away to college (initially at the Christian University in Abilene, Texas, but soon moving on to York College, in Nebraska), and Buddy had become a successful record star. There had been talk of marriage, but she decided that the lifestyle of the wife of a musician would be incompatible with her religious beliefs. At York College, Echo met and fell for a fellow student, Ron Griffith, who shared her religious views. She broke the news to Buddy at the end of 1957, and married Ron on St Valentine's Day in 1958. By then, just five years after he had started going steady with Echo, Buddy Holly's world had changed dramatically.

Prior to 1953, Lubbock's only local radio station was KSEL, a 'something for everyone' station which included pop, C&W and talk shows. The main country component was the *Saturday-Night Jamboree*, on which local bands played live in front of an audience. The station's general manager, David Pinkston, who deejayed under the name 'Pappy Dave Stone', was eager to expand the coverage of country music, but frustrated by KSEL's policy of trying to please everybody with a little bit of everything. When it was announced that a licence for a second station serving the area was coming up for auction, Stone, egged on by his country-loving DJ Ben Hall, managed to obtain financial backing for an all-country station, KDAV, which he set up using virtually all the staff from KSEL. It began broadcasting in September 1953, the month Buddy Holly turned seventeen, as the first all-country-music station in the USA. One of the people who moved from KSEL with Pappy Dave was a very tall broadcaster and talent scout christened William Duncan, but known to everyone as 'Hi Pockets' because, logically enough, of the length of his legs.

Ben Hall had already come across Buddy Holly at KSEL, when the sixteen-year-old Buddy turned up at the station unannounced trying to blag his way on air. He didn't succeed, but Hall, a songwriter and performer himself, was sufficiently impressed to use

Buddy occasionally as a member of his backing band at live gigs. Towards the end of September 1953, Hi Pockets checked out the Buddy and Jack duo at one of the Saturday morning gigs. Also impressed, he tried them out at a local show he was organising, then offered them a fifteen-minute appearance on KDAV's *Sunday Party*. On 4 November 1953 they performed, live, 'Your Cheatin' Heart', 'Got You on My Mind', 'I Couldn't Keep From Crying', and 'I Hear the Lord Callin' For Me'. The last of these was a Jack Neal composition. Of course, no fee was involved; Buddy and Jack were just grateful for the chance to reach a wider audience. The response of that audience was so enthusiastic that Pappy Dave turned over the entire half-hour slot to them, renaming it *Buddy and Jack's Sunday Party*. On 10 November, thrilled at the opportunity to play with the equipment in a brand-new radio station, Buddy and Jack recorded an acetate of 'I Hear the Lord Callin' For Me' and another Neal original, 'I Saw the Moon Cry Last Night'. Neal kept the recordings for decades, eventually allowing their release. The two songs can be found, along with the early home recordings mentioned at the end of Chapter One, on *Gotta Roll*, a compilation of Holly's early recordings released by Rev-Ola on CD in 2006.

The success of the *Sunday Party* attracted other musicians, including Bob Montgomery and Don Guess. Various combinations of these and other musicians joined up with Buddy and Jack on air, and performed locally, occasionally even being paid. In one combination, they were briefly known as the Rhythm Playboys – Buddy, Bob and Don. Another frequent visitor to KDAV was Sonny Curtis, who hailed from the nearby town of Meadow, where he had been born on 9 May 1937. Curtis had an impeccable musical background. He was the second youngest of six children from a dirt-poor family, a musical child prodigy who accompanied his older brothers Pete and Dean on fiddle as 'The Curtis Brothers' at local jamborees and radio stations from the age of ten. His uncles, the Mayfield Brothers, were also professional musicians, one of whom, Edd Mayfield, became a member of Bill Monroe's band in the 1950s. Curtis could also play a mean guitar. He had appeared with his brothers on KSEL, and later performed on KDAV both as a member of the *Sunday Party* and with Ben Hall.

Like Curtis, Buddy would play anywhere, for anyone who asked him. As his musical skills developed and he became increasingly influenced by R&B, in 1954 he switched from acoustic guitar to his first solid-body electric guitar, a Gibson Les Paul Gold Top. The musical obsession also took its toll on his school work, which went into a steep decline after years of being a model student academically, to the point where there began to be doubts about whether he would actually graduate from high school.

Jack Neal had different problems. Although only a couple of years older than Buddy, he had a steady job as an electrical contractor, and a steady girlfriend. Towards the end of 1954, he got married and moved to Ruidoso, New Mexico, giving up the prospect (such as it was) of a musical career. The obvious thing to do was for Bob Montgomery to replace Jack as Buddy's partner at KDAV, with the show duly renamed *The Buddy and Bob Sunday Party*; in fact, they were a trio, since Larry Welborn became their regular bass player both on air and when they performed locally as Buddy and Bob. Other musicians, including Don Guess, continued to sit in on a casual basis.

In the notes accompanying the 2004 CD *Stay All Night*, Welborn, who turned sixteen in April 1955, recalled how he was recruited by Buddy and Bob while playing guitar in a group called Cal Wayne and the Riverside Ranch Hands. The duo went along to see the band, and during one of the breaks Welborn took a ride with them in the car. 'They asked me if I could play bass. Well, I figured, if I could play guitar I could play bass. So I borrowed a bass fiddle from Lubbock High School and joined Buddy and Bob. We played a lot of country, and then rockabilly and later rock and roll.' Born in 1939, Welborn was still in junior high when he joined the act.

About the time that Buddy and Jack were meta-morphosing into Buddy and Bob, Sonny Curtis also became a regular part of the line-up. Buddy and Bob were still playing a lot of bluegrass music, with Buddy on banjo or mandolin, although his guitar style was becoming influenced by R&B. Curtis was a more sophisticated guitarist, already into jazz, who added another influence to the Holly style. He was also, like Montgomery and Don Guess, already writing songs, something that Holly, who still stayed in the background vocally, had barely attempted.

But everything changed on 2 January 1955, the day the Texan country boys saw a new performer called Elvis Presley in action, at a show promoted by KDAV which also included Carl Perkins and a young singer called Johnny Cash. Elvis's first single, 'Blue Moon of Kentucky'/'That's All Right Mama', had arrived at KDAV a few weeks ahead of the man him-self, but even that outrageous combination of a

country song written by Bill Monroe on one side of
the disc and a white man singing black R&B on the
other hardly prepared Lubbock for what was about
to hit them. Sonny Curtis still had the image fresh in
his mind 40 years later, when he was interviewed by
Philip Norman: '[Elvis] had on an orange sport coat,
red pants, white bucks. Tell you what boy, he looked
like a motorsickle headlight comin' right at you!'
The music was equally spectacular, while Presley's
on-stage gyrations horrified the parents present as
much as they delighted the squealing teenage girls
in the audience. And Elvis was still not quite twenty,
less than two years older than Buddy.

As Curtis admitted in his song 'The Real Buddy
Holly Story', at the time he didn't quite get where
Elvis was coming from. But Buddy did, and the bluegrass music was abandoned literally overnight. The
next day, the band became what Curtis later called
'Elvis clones', with Buddy the undoubted leader.
Even though he didn't really dig the music at the
time, Sonny was happy enough to make the change,
he later recalled, because of the effect the new music
had on the girls in the audience (*The Real Buddy Holly
Story*). Sonny himself, who had been playing fiddle,
switched to acoustic guitar and learned to play like
Elvis' guitarist, Scotty Moore; Buddy, previously

relatively restrained on stage as instrumentalist and second vocalist, became a much wilder front man, favouring electric guitar rather than banjo, developing his own vocal style by adding Elvis to his influences. From now on, although still shy and quiet off-stage, he became completely uninhibited in front of an audience. The change when he went on stage, several people have commented, was like flicking a switch to make a light come on.

On 13 February, Elvis was back in Lubbock as part of another show, still far from being top of the bill. This time, the opening act for the show was a local group – Buddy and Bob (and Larry and Sonny). KDAV's Ben Hall had just acquired an 8mm movie camera, and the silent colour film he took of the performers backstage survives – in one of the earliest colour films of Elvis, he is rubbing shoulders with Buddy Holly, although there is some doubt about the exact date this occurred. Elvis returned to Lubbock to perform several times in 1955. Sometimes Buddy and his friends watched from the audience, sometimes they got a spot low on the bill. They became firm friends with Elvis, and would try to entertain him by showing him the sights of Lubbock. This didn't provide much in the way of the kind of entertainment Elvis and other rock stars would later become known for; on one occasion, they took him to see the Jane Russell/Marilyn Monroe film *Gentlemen Prefer Blondes*, which was playing downtown.

Against this background, Buddy was still a senior at LHS, due to graduate in May 1955. But school didn't get much of a look-in (and nor did Echo!). When they weren't actually performing or rehearsing, Buddy, Bob, Sonny and Larry would use all the money they had been able to scrape up from their paid gigs and doing odd jobs, often working with L.O. Holley on construction sites in vacations, to pay for recording sessions. Some of these took place at KDAV, but from late 1954 through to the summer of 1955 most of them happened at the Nesman Recording Studios, 100 miles from Lubbock, in Wichita Falls – just up the road, as Texans measure distance.

These recordings, laid down on tape but not converted to disc at the time, were issued much later both in their original form and with unnecessary overdubbing. They intriguingly cover the transition from country to rock, or rockabilly as it became known. Montgomery songs such as 'Flower of My Heart' and 'Soft Place in My Heart' show their country roots, while at the other extreme 'Baby It's Love' and 'Down the Line' (both listed as Montgomery-Holly contributions, although Buddy's mother Ella actually provided some of the lyric on 'Baby It's Love') show the Elvis influence. The recordings were made as live performances, including vocals, with no multi-tracking or overdubbing at the time, and give a real flavour of what it must have been like to hear Buddy and Bob live. One song they didn't record, but which was popular at live shows, was Hank Ballard's 'Work With Me, Annie', one of Buddy's favourites, which was banned from most white radio stations, including KDAV, because of its sexually explicit lyrics.

Buddy and Bob were able to pay for these recording sessions in no small measure because they began to get paid more frequently for performing. At first, they'd been happy to play for anyone who could provide an audience, often in return for nothing more than a meal. Hi Pockets Duncan, disgusted at the way what he regarded as his boys were getting ripped off, offered to act as their manager. A formal contract was signed late in 1954, on the understanding that when the band became successful enough to work outside the immediate area, Hi Pockets would give up his involvement with them.

On both sides, the operative word was *when* they became successful; everyone was sure it would happen sooner or later. As well as hustling to get the boys paid work, it may have been Hi Pockets who had pointed out the need to beef up their sound by adding a bass player. As a sign of their new professionalism, the trio had business cards made, giving the name of the band as 'Buddy and Bob' and describing their music as 'Western and Bop', but including all three of the band members' names in smaller type, as well as that of business manager Hi Pockets Duncan, with the KDAV address. Sonny Curtis came along a little later.

As well as the core of Holly, Montgomery, Curtis and Welborn, other musicians involved on different sessions at Nesman's included Don Guess (sometimes on steel guitar, sometimes, especially after Elvis had hit Lubbock, on string bass) and Weldon Myrick (another protégé of Ben Hall, who later became a big country star) on steel guitar. Curtis played fiddle on the earlier, country-style recordings, but can be heard on guitar on the Elvis-influenced numbers. And in June 1955, another name appears on the list – drummer Jerry (known as 'J.I.') Allison.

Once again, it was thanks to Elvis. Elvis had just added a drummer, D.J. Fontana, to his band, finally severing his links, as far as Nashville was concerned, with country. To devotees, country music simply didn't have drums – full stop. But if Elvis had drums, Buddy had to have a drummer. The obvious choice was J.I., a schoolmate nearly three years younger than Buddy (born on 31 August 1939, he was about the same age as Larry Welborn) but only a year behind him academically. Thanks partly to the influence of his mother, who was a teacher, Allison had started school the day after he turned five years old, and would graduate from high school when he was still only sixteen, in the summer of 1956.

Holly and Allison had known each other since the Allison family moved to Lubbock from Plainview in 1950. They were already friends with shared musical interests, and had played together, notably when Buddy used to sit in with Cal Wayne and the Riverside Ranch Hands, who had a regular paid gig at the 16th and Avenue J Club on weekends. Allison, who had (and has) a playful sense of humour to match his prodigious musical talent, was, by 1955, the star of the band, even though he wasn't legally old enough to be in the club. He already had wide experience, in spite of his youth, of playing in different kinds of bands, including jazz, country music, and pop. Holly and Allison had a feel for the music and for each other's playing that made Buddy's appearances with the Ranch Hands memorable, and J.I. was, like Buddy, an instant convert to rock 'n' roll

– much more so than Bob Montgomery and Sonny Curtis. Buddy and J.I. were musical soulmates who soon became firm friends. He leaped at the chance to join Buddy's band, forming, with Buddy, the core of what would become the Crickets. History does not record what Cal Wayne thought about seeing his star performer following Larry Welborn into the growing Buddy and Bob 'duo'.

By now, Buddy had graduated from high school and could concentrate on his music full-time, with considerable support from his parents. L.O. bought a new car, which Buddy had free use of as band transport, provided he helped out with the payments from the income he was getting from his shows. With J.I. enjoying his summer vacation from high school, and Echo McGuire having already left for Abilene, they also rehearsed for hours, with Buddy developing his unique style of playing rhythm and lead simultaneously on one guitar. They developed an almost instinctive communication, so that it seemed J.I. knew what Buddy was going to do next during a song, and was ready with an appropriate response, even if it hadn't been rehearsed. They also got to see performances by coloured artists, and meet them backstage, at a venue called the Cotton Club, now being run by Hi Pockets. The biggest impact came from the sensational Little Richard. The career and life of this flamboyantly homosexual wild rocker still looks outrageous even today, and it is impossible to imagine his impact on white country boys in 1955.

In the summer of 1955, Buddy also worked as a labourer with his brother Larry, who was building himself a house. Larry had a tiling business, and was away for three months on a job in Arizona while Buddy was making the transition from country to rock. He returned home to find his kid brother more mature, full of self-confidence, and a greatly improved musician. Larry Holley later told how he had taken Buddy along with him on a trip to pick up some tiles, and they stopped off at what turned out to be a 'coloured joint' in San Angelo to get a hamburger. It was early evening, the place was dead, but a small group of black musicians was setting up in the corner. Buddy got talking to them, and when they learned he was a musician he was invited to play. Larry described what happened next in his memoir *The Buddy I Knew!*:

Buddy said 'Don't mind if I do.' As soon as he hit his chord, the atmosphere started to change. It seems like, that was the best sounding guitar I had ever heard. He played 'Sexy Ways' and did it up brown. The band and all the others were spellbound, including me. I had no idea that Buddy was that good. They would not let him sit back down.

'While he's playing,' Larry told Philip Norman, 'people start crowding round him, and I see the owner get on the 'phone, and then more and more people start coming in. Suddenly little old joint isn't dead any more. Buddy made the whole place come alive!'

By this time, Buddy was so popular in Lubbock that some of the men became jealous of the effect his music had on their girlfriends and threatened to 'fix' him. Having an ex-Marine big brother came in handy. 'There were several times,' says Larry, 'that I went out there to make sure that nobody bothered Buddy.' On one occasion, Larry saw his brother perform in a 'battle of the bands' show in Lubbock. 'Buddy came from the side of the stage to the middle in one movement without seeming to move his feet at all, and hit his guitar, and right away the whole crowd went hog-wild.'

It was also in 1955 that Bill Haley's 'Rock Around the Clock', already released the year before as the B-side to 'Thirteen Women', hit the charts when it was featured in the movie *Blackboard Jungle*. It stayed at number one in the US for eight weeks in the summer of 1955, the first rock 'n' roll record to reach number one on the Billboard Charts, and established rock 'n' roll as a nationwide – indeed, international – phenomenon. It also led to what seemed at first like Buddy Holly's big break.

On 14 October 1955, riding the success of the record with a major tour, Bill Haley and the Comets appeared in Lubbock at the Fair Park Coliseum. A Nashville agent and talent scout called Eddie Crandall was travelling with the tour, and saw Buddy and Bob among the support acts for the Comets. He was sufficiently impressed by Buddy in particular to take a second look at him the following night, when they opened for a KDAV show that included Johnny Cash and Floyd Cramer, with Elvis Presley as the main attraction. Crandall suggested to 'Colonel' Tom Parker, by then managing Elvis, that he should take Buddy on, but the Colonel said Elvis was enough for him and suggested that Crandall should do something to help Buddy.

On 2 December, after making some soundings in Nashville, Crandall wrote to Pappy Dave at KDAV saying that he would have a go at finding Buddy a recording contract. The same day that Pappy Dave got the letter, a telegram arrived at KDAV from Crandall, asking him to get Buddy to cut four demo songs and send them to Nashville 'soon as possible air mail special'. The telegram included the instruction: 'Dont change his style at all.'

On 7 December, Holly, Curtis, Guess and Allison recorded four new songs at Nesman's – Larry Welborn couldn't get time off from school, but Allison and Curtis, in their final year at LHS, had a more casual attitude to their formal education. It's a sign of the way the musical wind was blowing that Bob Montgomery didn't take part in the session. 'Don't Come Back Knockin'' and 'Love Me' were written by Holly in collaboration with a local songwriter called Sue Parrish. The other two, 'Baby Won't You Come Out Tonight' and 'I Guess I Was Just A Fool', were his first recorded solo compositions.

The songs hit Nashville at exactly the right time. Every record company wanted its own Elvis, and every publishing company wanted someone to write the sort of songs Elvis was having hits with. It was Holly's songwriting skill that first attracted attention. In the middle of January 1956, Crandall phoned Hi Pockets to tell him that Jim Denny, the owner of a Nashville publishing company called Cedarwood, would offer Buddy a songwriting contract and try to find a record company for him. Soon, the news got even better. Denny was able to persuade Paul Cohen, of Decca, to record Buddy.

This was potentially huge – Decca was one of the biggest companies in the record business, with a large roster of country stars. They were also Bill Haley's record label. The snag was that the offer of a recording contract was for Buddy only. Paul Cohen wanted a solo artist, and there was no room for Bob Montgomery. Buddy's initial reaction was to tell Bob that he would stand by his friend and tell Decca that it was both of them or nothing. But Bob quickly persuaded him that it was too good an opportunity to miss, and that he didn't mind being left out. In fact, the writing had been on the wall for some time. In the bluegrass days, Bob had clearly been the leading force and main singer, but by 1956 Buddy was the main singer, lead guitarist and front man. Bob graciously dropped out of the group to pursue his own career, becoming a very successful songwriter, record producer and music publisher.

Larry Welborn also decided not to pursue a career as a professional musician in Buddy's band. He was too young to leave school, and decided to form his own group, playing lead guitar with the Four

Teens. This left Buddy, Sonny and Don, with Bob Montgomery coming along for the ride and to offer moral support, to set out for Nashville in L.O.'s Oldsmobile at the end of January. J.I. was stuck in school. But at least Buddy was well equipped instrumentally for the event.

In preparation for touring and the recording session, Buddy had asked his brother Larry for a loan to buy new equipment and stage clothes. Larry, whose tiling business was going well, asked how much Buddy needed, thinking it might be 50 or 60 dollars. He was staggered when Buddy asked for a thousand. This was serious money in 1956, but Buddy assured Larry that he knew what he was doing. He had to have the best of everything, now that he was going to be a star, and the money would soon be paid back. Larry was won over, and provided the financial backing Buddy needed.

In several interviews, Larry recalls that $600 went on a guitar alone – a Fender Stratocaster from Adair's music store in Lubbock. This may be an exaggeration, since the going price for a Strat in those days should have been about half that, but it was still what Larry called 'a pile of money'. It was Buddy Holly who made the Stratocaster, previously favoured largely by country musicians, the instrument of choice for rock guitarists – for many years, Eric Clapton's main guitar was a 1956 Strat. More money went on an amplifier (perhaps the $600 included the amp) and the clothing, which included a red jacket, a green jacket, colourful shirts and, inevitably, a pair of blue suede shoes. Now it would be Buddy Holly who looked 'like a motorsickle headlight comin' right at you!'

Decca had given the job of producing Buddy Holly to Owen Bradley, who worked at his own studio, known as Bradley's Barn. Unfortunately, the injunction 'Don't change his style at all' hadn't filtered down that far. The session, which was something of an audition, since Buddy hadn't yet signed a contract with Decca, took place on 26 January. The musicians were Sonny Curtis on lead guitar, Don Guess on upright bass, and two Nashville session men, Grady Martin and Doug Kirkham, on rhythm guitar and drums respectively. The seasoned pros made no attempt to hide their disdain for the Texans. Buddy wasn't even allowed to play, handing over his brand-new Strat to Sonny, who says he became the first guitarist to use a Fender Stratocaster on a record.

Four songs were recorded in about three hours on the evening of 26 January – the familiar 'Love Me' and 'Don't Come Back Knockin'', plus 'Midnight Shift', a song by Earl Lee and Jimmy Ainsworth that featured the further adventures of Annie from 'Work With Me, Annie', and a Ben Hall original, 'Blue Days, Black Nights'. Buddy is clearly uncomfortable and unusually restrained on these tracks, compared with the ebullience of the Nesman's recordings. 'Blue Days, Black Nights' in particular could have been ideal for him if he had sung it in a deeper voice, with more feeling and a softer backing. Eventually, in April, this track would be issued as Buddy's first single, with 'Love Me' as the B-side. But one firm thing did soon come out of the first Nashville session – Buddy's professional name. His contract, dated 8 February 1956, was the one on which his name was spelled 'Holly'. The day after the Bradley's Barn session, Elvis Presley's 'Heartbreak Hotel', his first Nashville recording and first number one, was released. It would be the best-selling single of 1956.

While Elvis went from strength to strength, Buddy Holly went back to very nearly the old routine. As J.I. put it, 'Buddy got a record contract, went to Nashville and made some records, one was released, and in no time at all, we were back playing at the roller-rink' (Tobler). It wasn't quite that bad. The release of Buddy's first single in April did nothing to set the world of music on fire, but it did help to secure him a place on a tour with a 'Grand Ole Opry Show' travelling outside the West Texas area. The stars were Sonny James, Faron Young, Tommy Collins and Wanda Jackson. Buddy Holly and the Two-Tones, Sonny Curtis and Don Guess (who got their name because one wore a blue shirt and the other an orange shirt), were an 'extra added attraction', along with Carl Perkins. As such, they didn't even get seats on the tour bus, but had to follow along in their car. 'We were pretty terrible', Sonny Curtis told John Goldrosen. But, true to his word, as Buddy made the breakout from the Lubbock area with this tour and the recording deal, Hi Pockets Duncan tore up his contract with Buddy. For better or worse, Buddy was now a free agent.

'Blue Days, Black Nights' did at least get a good review in *Billboard*, which famously said: 'If the public will take more than one Presley or Perkins, as it well may, Holly stands a strong chance.' But Decca made no effort to promote the single, which sold only about 18,000 copies. Another record, made at Bradley's Barn in May 1956, was rather more successful – Gene Vincent's 'Be-Bop-A-Lula'. In spite of the lack of success with 'Blue Days, Black Nights', Paul Cohen was willing to try again, and invited

Buddy back to Nashville in July 1956 to record some more songs. Partly in preparation for this, as well as playing as many local gigs as they could around Lubbock, including at Hi Pockets' Cotton Club, Buddy recorded seven songs between February and April 1956 at a studio in Clovis run by a musician and producer called Norman Petty.

Holly had known of the existence of the studio since at least 1954, when Don Guess made a suggestion, never followed up, that the then Rhythm Playboys might record there. He had also learned about the quality of these facilities from other struggling West Texas performers, including Roy Orbison, who cut the first version of 'Ooby Dooby' there. As well as the quality of the studios, there was another attraction. Instead of charging artists by the hour to make recordings, Petty charged a flat fee of $75 for each pair of tracks laid down, no matter how long it took to get the sound right. Artists could take away acetates of their recordings at $3 each.

Clovis is only about 90 miles north-west of Lubbock, just across the border in New Mexico, so it was an easy drive for Buddy, Sonny, Don and J.I. At this time, the relationship with Norman Petty was purely one of customer and client. Buddy, J.I. and Don made no impact on the producer at all. But as it happened, Petty had just lost the guitarist from his own trio, and was sufficiently impressed by Sonny Curtis to offer him the job. Curtis thought he'd made it, until he was auditioned and realised that the Norman Petty Trio was essentially a kind of cabaret act playing mood music on the supper club circuit. 'So I turned it down,' Curtis told Philip Norman, 'and after that, I don't believe Norman [Petty] liked me until the day he died.'

Significantly, six of the songs recorded in Clovis at those sessions were Holly originals – 'Baby Won't You Come Out Tonight', 'Because I Love You', 'Changing All Those Changes', 'I Guess I Was Just A Fool', 'I'm Gonna Set My Foot Down' and 'Rock-a-Bye Rock'. The seventh track, 'It's Not My Fault', was written by Ben Hall and Weldon Myrick. Within a few weeks, and tantalisingly for us just too late to be included in these sessions, another Holly composition, this time a collaboration with Jerry Allison, was added to their repertoire.

From 31 May to 20 June 1956, the western *The Searchers*, directed by John Ford and starring John Wayne, was the main movie attraction in Lubbock. Buddy, Sonny Curtis and Jerry Allison watched it together, and picked up the phrase used repeatedly in the movie by the John Wayne character to express his determination to overcome obstacles in the search for his niece, kidnapped by what in those days were called Red Indians. Whenever someone suggests he isn't tough enough to deal with a problem and ought to give up, he growls, 'That'll be the day.' The phrase became part of the trio's everyday language. So when Buddy went over to J.I.'s house a few days later with an idea for a tune and suggested that the two of them write a song together, J.I., who had never tried to write a song before, responded jokingly, 'That'll be the day.' Buddy laughed, and picked up on the phrase. They wrote the song in less than half an hour, making up alternate lines.

Decca had enough faith in Buddy to schedule another recording session at Bradley's Barn on 22 July 1956, and by this time Jerry Allison and Sonny Curtis were both out of school for good and able, with Don Guess, to accompany Buddy. Owen Bradley agreed to let Holly play rhythm guitar on the session, so it was the regular team, with no session musicians, who recorded a Sonny Curtis original, 'Rock Around With Ollie Vee', a Holly composition, 'I'm Changing All Those Changes', 'That'll Be The Day', a Don Guess song titled 'Girl On My Mind', and 'Ting-a-Ling', written by Ahmet Ertegun, who later became the head of Atlantic Records. It's a sign of how much faith Holly had in the new Holly–Allison collaboration that they did nineteen takes of 'That'll Be The Day', but the result was still unsatisfactory. Buddy wasn't even allowed to sing it naturally – he was encouraged to sing in a higher register than he was used to, to make a more 'country' sound. Buddy sings too high, the band is mixed too far in the background, and there is a ridiculous amount of echo. Apart from 'That'll Be The Day', most attention at the session focused on 'Rock Around With Ollie Vee', which after eight takes was an entirely presentable example of rockabilly, clearly the most commercial recording, though not the best song, to emerge from the session.

When Decca needed a name for Holly's backing group, 'Two-Tones' obviously wouldn't work, so they became, on paper, 'Buddy Holly and the Three Tunes'. Both names were purely administrative conveniences to fit the requirements of tour organisers or record companies. When Buddy performed other gigs, after the demise of Buddy and Bob he was always simply billed as 'Buddy Holly', whoever happened to be playing behind him on that particular occasion. In any case, it was the last time Buddy Holly and Sonny Curtis would record together. Sonny's family were too poor to support him now that he had graduated from high school, and he had to make a living. 'Buddy had great faith in the future,' says Sonny, 'but I honestly felt we weren't really going anywhere.' With no sign of Decca releasing any of the new recordings and only inter-mittent paid gigs with Buddy, when he was offered a chance to tour as a guitarist with Slim Whitman's band he jumped at it.

'That's just the way it was', Sonny told me. He had been working at a music store in Lubbock, sell-ing guitars and giving guitar lessons, and one of the people working with him was Sammy Hodge, who was a steel guitarist who had played with Slim Whit-man. Sammy introduced him to Whitman, who was looking for a guitar player for a tour, and Sonny went on the road with him. He later accepted a job playing in a club in Colorado Springs for $110 a week. Eventually, he became a successful singer/songwriter in his own right.

In any case, Sonny's situation in Buddy Holly's band was becoming uncomfortable. For a talented guitarist, increasingly proficient songwriter and decent vocalist, the prospect of playing rhythm while Buddy wrote most of the songs, sang, and increas-ingly chose to play lead cannot have been very appealing – although if he had been able to stay, perhaps a Holly–Curtis partnership like that of Lennon–McCartney might soon have emerged.

With no such prospect in sight, in the summer of 1956 Buddy worked with his brother Larry laying tiles, or with L.O. on house construction jobs. At every opportunity, he would get together with Jerry Allison to rehearse; J.I.'s drums became a permanent fixture in the Holley house, and the pair developed an instinctive feel for each other's playing, creating a full sound with just two people. Sometimes, Buddy and J.I. would play gigs as a duo, just drums and guitar but making a sound big enough to fill a dance hall, or the local roller rink, where they played regularly. Their frustration at failing to get a record off the ground and break out of their own area was intensified by the audience reaction on 24 August, when Little Richard played the Cotton Club again and provoked such enthusiasm among the mostly white audience that the show was stopped. It just wasn't seemly for white kids, especially girls, to be getting so excited about a black performer.

On 9 September, Elvis, who had so recently been the inspiration for Buddy's move towards rock' n' roll, appeared on the *Ed Sullivan Show* for the first time, attracting 54 million viewers. All this belatedly drew the attention of the Lubbock *Avalanche-Journal* to their local star. On 23 October they ran a story headlined 'Young Singer is Lubbock's "Answer to Elvis Presley"', including the 'news' of Buddy's recording contract with Decca. But they reassured readers that he wasn't too outrageous:

> Holly, who has a three piece orchestra just like Presley's, has reverted to playing and singing rock 'n' roll exclusively. He plays an electric standard guitar and wears 'fancy' sports coats for his singing engagements, but the resemblance to the widely known entertainer ends there. Holly refuses to wear one of the bright sports coats on the street, even for publicity.

But the nearest that Lubbock's answer to Elvis Presley got to fame that autumn was a third and, as it turned out, final recording session with Decca, on 15 November. This time, only Don Guess went along with him to Nashville, with the pair of them taking a long detour to York, Nebraska, for Buddy to fit in a fleeting visit to Echo. At this session, Don played with Harold Bradley, Grady Martin, Floyd Cramer and Farris Coursey, while Buddy was once again only allowed to sing. On one track, a new version of 'Rock Around With Ollie Vee', they were joined by E.R.

'Dutch' McMillin on tenor saxophone. Just two other tracks were recorded – a Guess–Neal composition, 'Modern Don Juan', and a solo Guess composition, 'You Are My One Desire'. Once again, 'Rock Around With Ollie Vee' sounds to modern ears like the stand-out track; but Decca chose to release the other two tracks, with 'Modern Don Juan' as the A-side, on, of all days, Christmas Eve 1956. It was almost as though they were trying to ensure that the record would be a flop so they could get rid of Holly. Sure enough, early in the New Year he received a letter informing him that the one-year contract, which expired on 26 January, the anniversary of the first Nashville session, would not be renewed.

Some time after the third Nashville session and the arrival of this letter, Buddy recorded the songs 'Gone' and 'Have You Ever Been Lonely' with Jerry Allison and (probably) Don Guess, at home in Lubbock. Around the same time, he made home recordings of several rock 'n' roll standards accompanied by Allison on drums, Larry Holley on guitar, and an unknown bass player; in spite of the rawness of these recordings, they show the real Buddy Holly, and highlight the incompetence of Decca in failing to let him loose in Nashville. The tracks were 'Brown Eyed Handsome Man', 'Good Rockin' Tonight', 'Rip it Up', 'Blue Monday', the instrumental 'Honky Tonk', 'Blue Suede Shoes', 'Shake, Rattle and Roll', 'Bo Diddley', 'Ain't Got No Home', and another instrumental, 'Holly Hop', which should really be 'Holley Hop', since it was based on a tune Ella Holley had made up that Buddy heard his mother whistling around the house. There were enough tracks to have made a great album, if they'd been recorded under proper studio conditions, but with the same freedom. Indeed, I have this set as a playlist on my iPod; they sound so much better together than the way they were eventually released, scattered across several posthumous Buddy Holly albums with various Norman Petty tweaks.

In January 1957, Buddy and the Two-Tones (including J.I., according to his own recollection, who had enrolled at Texas Tech but quit college to take the gig) toured for a couple of weeks at the bottom of the bill on a package headed by Hank Thompson and including George Jones, shortly before Sonny Curtis left for Colorado Springs. They were paid $10 a day each, plus expenses. Don Guess also decided he'd had enough after this tour, becoming a session musician for a time before giving up music for the insurance business. He made two unsuccessful singles, notable because the B-side of his first record, released by Brunswick in November 1958, is a track called 'Just A Little Lovin' Baby' which bears a remarkable resemblance to Boots Randolph's 1963 hit 'Yakety Sax', a tune familiar to many as the Benny Hill theme.

That left Buddy and J.I. What else could they do but head back to Norman Petty's studio in Clovis to record some more demos?

CHAPTER THREE

That'll Be The Day

Norman Petty is both the hero and the villain of the Buddy Holly story. The hero because he provided the opportunity for Holly to make hit recordings; the villain because his greed and selfishness were directly responsible for Holly undertaking his fatal last tour. But at first, what mattered was his musical expertise and the studio facilities he provided in Clovis. Whatever happened later, it should never be forgotten that his role was as important in developing Buddy Holly as a recording artist as George Martin was to the Beatles.

Petty was a complicated and secretive man. He had much to be secretive about, since he was gay, and very firmly in the closet in bigoted 1950s New Mexico (where the word 'gay' certainly didn't have its modern meaning). But he had a superb musical ear, and it was said that hearing a false note caused him physical pain. Born in Clovis in 1927, Petty was only nine years older than Buddy, and still not 30 when they met. Thanks to his sensitivity to music, even as a child he had been able to play tunes on the piano after hearing them only once, and he never had to learn to read music – he could feel it. He soon put the skill to good use by getting part-time work as a piano tuner. Petty was also fascinated with the technology of musical recording. As a teenager, he worked as a DJ on KICA in Clovis, and made recordings with his first group, the Torchy Swingsters, on a wire recorder – very advanced technology for the day. Always alert to any financial possibilities, Petty also bought a disc-cutting machine, on which local people could record greetings on 78 rpm acetates to send to relations – for a fee.

In high school, Petty met a girl called Violet Ann Brady, who shared his musical interests and could both read and write music. Petty was just too young to see military service in World War Two, but still had to do his spell in the armed forces, never getting farther afield than Norfolk, Virginia. In 1948, after his military service, he married Vi. He was 21 and she was twenty. Together with guitarist Jack Vaughn, they formed the Norman Petty Trio, finding a comfortable niche as touring performers, popular at the many US Air Force bases in New Mexico, and scoring two hits, 'Mood Indigo' in 1954 and the instrumental 'Almost Paradise' in 1957. It was the royalties from 'Mood Indigo' that paid for Petty's studio, full of state-of-the-art technology and including an Ampex reel-to-reel tape recorder, the kind of machine which had previously been the almost exclusive preserve of the military. The studio, built in a converted store next to the gas station owned by his parents, was small; but thanks to Petty's sensitive ear it had superb acoustics, and instead of using a tape delay to produce an artificial echo effect it would soon have a genuine echo chamber – an empty room in which sound from a speaker literally echoed off the walls before being picked up by a microphone and recorded.

Perhaps Petty's most striking innovation was to take his Ampex machine along with him when the trio was on tour, setting it up in some convenient corner of the officers' club on an airbase to make studio-quality recordings while on the road.

The professional set-up included a music publishing company, NorVaJak, named from the Christian names of the original trio (Vaughn, as I have mentioned, left just about the time Buddy came on the scene, leading Petty to offer Sonny Curtis the job of guitarist with the trio). To help run his businesses,

Petty employed Norma Jean Berry as his secretary and book-keeper. Even at the time, friends and business colleagues felt that the relationship between Norman and Vi was essentially a professional one, and the gossip was heightened by the presence in the Petty entourage of Norma Jean, who conformed in both style and mannerisms to the stereotypical image of a butch lesbian. The private life of the Pettys shouldn't be relevant to the story of Buddy Holly's music, but it's worth mentioning since it sheds some insight into why Petty was the complicated, sometimes contradictory person he was, which certainly did affect his relationship with Buddy. What comes across as selfishness and greed may be partly explained by a need for security in a society hostile to his lifestyle.

NorVaJak was the key to the financial success of the whole business. Petty knew how important it was for musicians to feel relaxed and be comfortable in the studio, without time pressure on them. He presented them with an opportunity for freedom of expression that remained unique in the recording industry until the Beatles came along and changed everything; but he got something in return. Musicians could spend as long as they liked perfecting a record, provided that they published their songs with NorVaJak, and preferably cut Norman Petty in as co-composer, whether he had actually contributed to the writing or not.

For a struggling band or singer, this was no bad deal. They risked nothing, and if they got a hit, well, half of something was better than all of nothing. For Petty, it meant that he could subsidise the recording of a lot of flops, paid for by the royalties that came in from the occasional hit, and make money for himself as well. In many ways, it was a satisfactory business arrangement. But Petty would push it to extremes.

Some idea of his character comes from an interview Larry Holley gave to Philip Norman:

> During World War Two, when I was in the military over in Saipan, I remember falling asleep one night in a fox-hole … when I woke up in the fox-hole, there was this giant snail crawling right across my face … Well, I tell you, I used to get just the same kind of feeling every time I was around Norman Petty.

There are many stories of how Petty could appear superficially generous and charming, treating his session musicians or backing singers to lunch, but how difficult it was to get him to part with money he actually owed them. And by all accounts, Hi Pockets Duncan, when he heard Buddy was recording in Clovis, advised him in no uncertain terms that recording demos there was all very well, but he shouldn't get into any business relationship with Petty. But half of something is better than all of nothing – as long as you get your half.

Ironically, another aspect of Petty's complex character led to him missing out on what could have been the first big pot of gold for himself and NorVaJak. In 1956, a West Texas group called the Rhythm Orchids used Petty's studio to record a couple of demos, including the song 'Party Doll', which had been written by the singer, Buddy Knox. It's a sign of Petty's willingness to innovate that the drummer on the track is actually playing a cardboard box. The recording had obvious commercial potential, but even Norman Petty could not bring himself to be associated with it. The problem was that Petty, sharing the religious sensibilities of a slightly older generation, was uncomfortable with the whole idea of a song about a 'party doll', especially one which included the repeated line 'I'll make love to you'. God forbid that his name should be associated with this. He didn't even try to get a credit as co-composer, and let the Rhythm Orchids take their master tapes away to do what they wanted with them.

Before too long, the songs attracted the attention of Roulette Records in New York, who hit upon the cunning plan of releasing 'Party Doll' under the name Buddy Knox and another track from the Clovis session, 'I'm Sticking With You', under the name of Jimmy Bowen, another member of the band, who sang lead on it. Both were hits, 'Party Doll' reaching number one in March 1957 and 'I'm Sticking With You' number eleven in April. With Buddy Knox being very much the one that got away, Petty took far more notice of Buddy Holly than he had previously when Buddy arrived in Clovis to record a couple of demos at the end of January 1957, after the Hank Thompson tour and the breakup of the 'Three Tunes'. He was accompanied by Jerry Allison, by Larry Welborn, fitting in the session as a favour between his other commitments, and with Larry Holley coming along to provide moral support and help with the driving.

The songs Buddy had chosen to record were two stalwarts of his stage act that are the very essence of rock 'n' roll. 'Brown Eyed Handsome Man' was a Chuck Berry song, released in 1956 as the B-side of his R&B hit single 'Too Much Monkey Business'. 'Bo Diddley' was the signature tune of the eponymous artist, released as his first single in 1955, with 'I'm a Man' on the other side; it stayed on the R&B chart for eighteen weeks. Buddy Holly was fascinated by the rhythm used by Bo Diddley on most of his records – the 'Bo Diddley beat' – and as well as his recording of 'Bo Diddley' itself, there is a surviving tape of a rehearsal session with him and J.I. perfecting the instrumental for another Diddley song, 'Mona'. Tantalisingly, there is one almost complete take of the song, but with Buddy singing along quietly off-mike, so that his voice can barely be heard. He also later used the rhythm as the basis for his song 'Not Fade Away' (the Rolling Stones' first US release), and more subtly in his song 'Love's Made A Fool Of You'.

The raw versions of 'Bo Diddley' and 'Brown Eyed Handsome Man' recorded in Clovis early in 1957 are the nearest thing we have to the excitement of a live Buddy Holly performance, and for me 'Brown Eyed Handsome Man' is the essence both of Holly and of rock 'n' roll – two kids, one still in his teens, the other barely twenty, having fun and not only producing a great sound, but outdoing Chuck Berry on a Chuck Berry song! And nothing better encapsulates the contribution Jerry Allison made to the Buddy Holly sound.

Carl Bunch, the drummer who played with Buddy on his last tour and had the task of trying to replicate J.I.'s sound, has said that J.I. invented what became rock drumming. Before him, people like Bill Haley had drummers who provided a strict 2/4 or 4/4 back-beat, and nothing else; J.I. played the drums like a lead instrument, developing a whole new rhythm pattern, originating with 'Bo Diddley'.

It's no surprise that when overdubbed versions of the songs were eventually released in the UK in 1963, 'Brown Eyed Handsome Man' went to number three in March (shortly before the Beatles hit number one with 'From Me to You'), and 'Bo Diddley' went to number four in June. It's also hardly surprising that Norman Petty took notice of the sound that the gangly Texan kids, casually dressed in white T-shirts and jeans, were laying down in his studio. He told them to come back at the end of February with a couple of original songs, and he would help them to make a professional-quality demo to show to the big record companies.

After the disappointment of the Nashville sessions, Buddy determined to pull out all the stops to make the best possible recordings this time. Among the circle of musicians in and around Lubbock was Gary Tollett, a cousin of the Rhythm Orchids' guitarist Donnie Lanier, who was eager to follow Donnie into the big time (he eventually recorded, unsuccessfully, under the name Gary Dale). In exchange for Buddy and J.I. helping out at a recording session for Gary at KDAV, Gary and his wife Ramona offered to provide backing vocals for Buddy's forthcoming Clovis session, along with Niki Sullivan, who had also been present at the KDAV session. Still convinced that 'That'll Be The Day' had potential, Buddy chose the number for some intensive rehearsals with the new line-up, during which the song was transformed. At the last minute he wrote a second song, 'I'm Lookin' For Someone To Love', for the session (he completed the song in the car on the way to Clovis, putting in the lines 'drunk man, street car – foot slip, there you are' when Larry Holley reminded him of this saying that their mother used).

On 24 February 1957 Buddy, J.I. and the Tolletts piled into Buddy's latest car, a red '55 Cadillac largely paid for by Larry Holley, and on this occasion driven by him as well, and headed for Clovis; Niki Sullivan and Larry Welborn, once again helping out as nobody else was available, made their way separately. Most of the evening session at Petty's studio was devoted to the new song, partly because it was intended as the A-side of any single, partly because there had been no opportunity to rehearse it. The recording was made like a live performance, with all the musicians and singers performing at the same time (Niki, Ramona and Gary shared a single mike). If anyone fluffed, the whole thing had to be done again. Around 3am, relaxed and in a party mood, they finally got around to 'That'll Be The Day', which they knew thoroughly from their extensive rehearsals, knocking out a satisfactory version in next to no time.

According to Gary and Ramona Tollett, 'there were three takes. The last of the three was used for the master. Everyone was getting tired as it was around 4:00 in the morning and everyone had to get back to Lubbock. Norman was pleased that we had done such a good job on such a short practice session. We had spent the night recording "Lookin' For Someone To Love", Buddy had thought that would be the A side, but history dictated otherwise!' 'We didn't try to get it perfect', J.I. told John Goldrosen. It was 'just a demo', and 'we never suspected that recording would come out'. On both tracks, the line-up was: Buddy Holly, guitar and vocal; Larry Welborn, upright bass; Jerry Allison, drums; Gary Tollett, Ramona Tollett and Niki Sullivan, backing vocals. Then, it was time to get down to business.

After listening to the playbacks, it was clear that 'That'll Be The Day' was the stronger of the two songs, and the one Petty should promote. For the studio time, his help on the session and the effort he intended to make to get the record released by a major company, Norman Petty demanded that his name be added as co-composer on both titles. In the case of 'That'll Be The Day' this was the most outrageous example of his entire career, since the song had already been recorded and published with the writing credit Allison–Holly. From now on, it would read Allison–Holly–Petty. With the songs being published by NorVaJak, Norman would be doubly rewarded financially if the record became a hit.

Petty had a smooth line to use on the naive boys from Lubbock. He told them that his name on the records would get them noticed by record company executives and DJs who had already heard of the Norman Petty Trio – as if a familiarity with 'Mood Indigo' would be likely to make a DJ spin 'That'll Be The Day'. But hey – 50 per cent of something is better than 100 per cent of nothing. Petty also didn't see any problem with the fact that publishing rights to 'That'll Be The Day' were actually owned by Cedarwood; he'd find a way round it. Indeed, in due course he astutely persuaded Cedarwood to swap those rights for the rights in another Holly song,

'Think It Over'. Good though the latter is, I know which one I'd rather own.

There was still the problem of the Nashville version of 'That'll Be The Day'. By the terms of his Nashville contract, Buddy wasn't allowed to re-record the song for anyone else. With the Clovis version in the can, on Thursday 28 February he made a long-distance phone call from J.I.'s parents' house to Paul Cohen at Decca to ask for permission to re-use the song. Clearly in the hope of having proof that permission had been granted, he recorded the conversation. It makes fascinating listening as Buddy, clearly uncomfortable at having to lie about the fact that he had already recorded the song again, absorbs the information that he can't legally re-record any of the songs he recorded for Decca for five years, even if Decca never did anything with them.

It was Petty who came up with a typically cunning solution to the problem. If the new version of 'That'll Be The Day' wasn't released under Buddy's name, there was little chance, he suggested, of anyone at Decca realising he was the singer. All they needed was a name for the band. Buddy Knox's name had been pulled out of the group name the Rhythm Orchids; Buddy Holly's name could be hidden within a group.

Buddy was a big fan of the black R&B group the Spiders, who, after a string of hits, had a single coupling 'Honey Bee' with 'That's My Desire' out in January 1957. Buddy's liking for the group led to a search through an encyclopaedia for other 'creepy crawly' names, and after rejecting (among others) the Beetles, they hit upon the Crickets, after an insect known for its chirpy 'music'. So when Norman Petty started touting the recording of 'That'll Be The Day' around the New York record companies, it was labelled as being by the Crickets.

While Petty got on with the business side of things, the newly-named Crickets got on with recording more songs, now with Niki Sullivan added as rhythm guitarist and a young musician called Joe B. Mauldin coming in on bass as a permanent member of the band.

Sullivan had already been playing with Buddy on some live performances, having graduated from being a fan (he described Buddy as 'the nearest thing to Elvis Presley we had' in Lubbock) to becoming part of the band. They got together late in 1956, when a mutual friend took the nineteen-year-old Niki along to a jam session at the Holley house. Sullivan didn't have a high opinion of his own skill as a guitarist, and was surprised but pleased when

Buddy and J.I. asked him to formally become one of the Crickets, soon after the 'That'll Be The Day' session. But he had a great stage presence, and his Elvis-like gyrations became a feature of the Crickets' act. Niki and Buddy were actually distant cousins, although they didn't know this at the time, and Niki bore a distinct physical resemblance to Buddy, even down to wearing a similar kind of glasses. The most influential rock band of all time actually had two bespectacled guitarists!

Larry Welborn didn't want to rejoin Buddy on a permanent basis, and at that time there was no reason, except Buddy's enthusiasm, for him to think that the latest recordings would result in any more success than the Nashville sessions, so he stayed fronting the Four Teens. According to J.I., Buddy and Larry were also beginning to irritate one another. When Larry wasn't available for a gig, the bass player from the Four Teens, Joe Benson Mauldin (always known as Joe B.) took his place. Just sixteen, Joe B. was no great bass player, but could put on a good show, giving the impression he was playing far more notes than he was actually plucking. He was also a rarity among the bass players Buddy knew in that he actually owned his own bass. That was enough to get him an invitation to join the Crickets, on the understanding that Larry Welborn didn't mind losing him from the Four Teens. Buddy told Joe B., who must surely have been one of the luckiest sixteen-year-old musicians of all time, that the Crickets were about to hit the big time on the back of 'That'll Be The Day'. Unimpressed, Joe B. said he would join the band on one condition – that he could keep his job as a butcher's assistant.

'Buddy was always the leader of our group', said Niki. 'Buddy had something in mind that, frankly, I don't think all of us quite understood. Buddy was looking for a sound to record.' (VH1)

As well as continuing to play live whenever there was an opportunity, the new line-up of Holly, Allison, Sullivan and Mauldin returned to Clovis on 1 March 1957 (the day 'Party Doll' hit number one) to provide backing for a Gary Tollett session and to record two of their own songs – 'Last Night', which Joe B. had written with the Four Teens but which became credited to Mauldin–Petty, and the first version of 'Maybe Baby', credited to Holly–Petty, which wouldn't be released in Holly's lifetime. Buddy got the idea for the title of 'Maybe Baby' from his mother. There were no more backing vocals from the Tolletts, though; from now on, although Niki provided second vocal on some recordings, including this version of 'Maybe Baby', Petty used a group of professional session singers, the Picks, adding their contribution later.

Through their contacts with Buddy Knox, the Crickets offered 'That'll Be The Day' to Roulette Records, who turned it down largely because they felt they were busy enough developing the various strands from the Rhythm Orchids. That left Norman Petty (who doesn't seem to have been aware of the approach to Roulette) as the main line of communication with New York. He had no more success with the record companies than they had, so he tried a different tack. NorVaJak had a publishing arrangement with the internationally renowned Peer–Southern publishing company, so Petty took the demo to their general manager, Murray Deutch. Deutch immediately felt there was something special about the record, and offered to use his influence to try to get the Crickets a recording deal – in exchange for half the publishing rights on 'That'll Be The Day' and 'I'm Lookin' for Someone to Love'. Norman agreed; he too knew that 50 per cent of something is better than all of nothing.

Even with Deutch behind it, 'That'll Be The Day' didn't get much response from the record companies in New York. The only offer came from Bob Thiele of

Coral Records. Through a bizarre twist of fate, Coral was a subsidiary of Decca, who had already rejected Buddy and who actually owned the rights to 'That'll Be The Day'. But Petty hadn't mentioned any of this to Deutch or Thiele. Nobody else at Coral liked the recording. It was completely unlike anything else on the label, which featured artists such as Debbie Reynolds and Teresa Brewer. Grudgingly, it was agreed to release the record on the even less prestigious Brunswick label, part of the Coral set-up, with an initial pressing of just 1,000 copies. Even 'Blue Days, Black Nights' had sold eighteen times that! But at least it was a deal. On 19 March 1957 (my eleventh birthday), Bob Thiele signed an agreement to purchase the two masters from the 24 February session for a derisory $100 advance. But Petty, astutely, squeezed a decent royalty rate of 5 per cent on the selling price of the records out of Coral, nearly twice the going rate for an unknown artist.

Petty took the contract to Clovis, where it was signed by Jerry Allison, Niki Sullivan and Joe B. Mauldin as the Crickets; Buddy's name was left off the contract as part of the smokescreen to confuse Decca in Nashville. When the smoke did clear, in view of the fact that Coral was a part of Decca, the situation was resolved by Buddy agreeing to waive the royalties due to him on the Nashville version of 'That'll Be The Day'. Things could have been tricky, though, had he sold the recording to another label such as Roulette. But as far as Coral were concerned, in March 1957 the Crickets seemed to be a three-piece band, and Buddy Holly didn't exist, except as a composer. By contrast, Joe B. now had an interest in a record he had taken no part in making, and Niki was generously rewarded for contributing no more than backing vocals! Larry Welborn got nothing, but never complained.

The income would be channelled through Norman Petty, who took 10 per cent off the top. Since the royalty rate was so generous, he suggested that the boys (he took to calling them his 'boys', even though he wasn't much older than Buddy) donate the difference between the 3 per cent royalty they might have expected and the 5 per cent they were actually getting as a tithe to their churches. The boys, all good Baptists, agreed, at a stroke giving away 40 per cent of their income to the church. Petty, of course, offered to take care of the tithing and pass on the remaining 60 per cent of their income to them. Or rather, to hold it in a special band account from which they could draw. Norman Petty was 'the cop, he was the policeman, and nobody could talk to any-

body unless Norman knew what it was all about ...
every song, he had to have billing as well as everybody else' (Murray Deutch, *The Real Buddy Holly
Story*).

Buddy had a different attitude to money. 'Buddy
was just a nice guy. He was a nice kid – he was a
gentleman, he really was' (Bob Thiele, *The Real
Buddy Holly Story*). He wanted to split everything
equally between the four members of the band, and
for live gigs that was the way things were until Niki
Sullivan left; afterwards, Buddy took 50 per cent and
the other two split the other 50 per cent. On record
royalties, he was persuaded by Petty to take two-
thirds of the income – but the other Crickets shared
their third even on records they hadn't played on,
such as 'Early In The Morning'.

Coral were in no hurry to release 'That'll Be The
Day', and if Buddy had been under contract to them
in the way he had been to Decca, he would have been
left kicking his heels and waiting for some action.
But he was still in the position of making his own
recordings independently with Norman Petty in
Clovis as and when he wanted to, then licensing the
masters to Coral. He had complete artistic freedom,
and he made good use of it by continuing to record
while waiting for some action at Coral. Petty, who

could smell the money, gave the Crickets all the recording time they wanted, fed them, and even provided overnight accommodation. In spite of his own musically square background, he genuinely liked the music, and found the experience of working with Buddy exhilarating. They were both perfectionists, and both loved music. At the time, that was all that mattered. And if Petty needed some backing musicians for a session, Buddy and the boys were happy to oblige – the best example is Holly's superb guitar work on Jack Huddle's otherwise unexceptional 'Starlight'.

It wasn't just the musicians who were impressed by Petty's apparent generosity. Larry Holley, along with Travis and L.O., was recruited to tile an attic space that became the Clovis studio's echo chamber, contributing to the Buddy Holly sound on records made after 'Maybe Baby' mark one. Of course, they weren't paid; it was a favour to thank Norman for all the work he was doing for Buddy.

In March 1957, Holly recorded a new song, 'Words of Love', in the studio in Clovis. In contrast to 'That'll Be The Day', this is a gentle love song, with Buddy using overdubbing for the first time. Buddy had two guitar parts that he wanted to play on the record, and the only way to do this at that time was to make one recording then literally record the second part over the top of it, playing the first recording from one tape machine to another while the extra voices or instruments were being recorded simultaneously onto the second tape. This was all done in mono, onto one single track. It was a technique that had been pioneered by Les Paul and Mary Ford, but Holly introduced it into rock, and made it his own. Once he had perfected the arrangement, a full recording was made on 8 April 1957. Drums, bass and rhythm guitar (Holly) plus vocal (Holly) were recorded first, then Holly added the lead guitar part and additional vocal in places, duetting with himself. This was known as double-tracking. Apart from the difficulty of singing and playing accurately so that there was a perfect musical match between the two recordings, this technique also required great skill on the part of the sound engineer, who had to adjust the volume levels of the two recordings so that they sounded as if they had all been recorded together. Petty did this beautifully.

At the same session, almost as a throwaway, Buddy, J.I. and Joe B. recorded 'Mailman, Bring Me No More Blues', with a grumpy Vi Petty thumping aggressively at the piano, annoyed at having been got out of bed to contribute. There was a good reason for recording this track; it had been co-written by Bob Thiele, under the pseudonym Stanley Clayton. The tapes were then despatched to Thiele, to demonstrate Holly's versatility.

Thiele was sufficiently impressed by the softer sound on 'Words of Love' that he proposed releasing it on the Coral label under Buddy's own name, having by now learned the identity of the singer on the Crickets' records. The success of the two spin-offs from the Rhythm Orchids may have encouraged Thiele to think along these lines, but in that case two different singers out of the same band were featured; uniquely, Buddy Holly would be releasing singles under his own name and as leader of the Crickets at the same time. Buddy signed with Coral under his own name on 16 May, leading to the inevitable confrontation with Decca and its satisfactory conclusion. This was still eleven days before the release of the Clovis version of 'That'll Be The Day'. Far from promoting the record, Brunswick didn't even bother to tell the band it had come out; Buddy found out only when he called New York to ask why nothing had happened, and was told it was already being played on the radio.

Larry Holley fills in some of the details about that phone call. He recalls that after Buddy had cut several records in Clovis, he was working as a helper in the tile business, and one day 'seemed to have the blues pretty bad'. When Larry asked why, he replied: 'I know I could make it if I just got a little bit of a push from somebody ... I just don't know what's going on.' So Larry said, 'OK, let's put up the tools, and go to mother's house, and make a phone call to New York.' When Deutch gave Buddy the news that the single had been released, his immediate response was: 'Well, could you send me $500, 'cause I'm broke?' And Deutch did. 'Well,' says Larry, 'I guess you know that I lost my helper pretty soon.'

'That'll Be The Day' was greeted by *Billboard* on 10 June as a 'fine vocal' that 'should get play ... Performance is better than material.' Astutely, it described 'I'm Lookin' For Someone To Love' as getting a 'bright, vigorous treatment, and should do as well as the flip'. Throughout his career, Buddy Holly / Crickets songs had B-sides powerful enough to be hits in their own right. But there was little immediate action in terms of sales.

But while 'That'll Be The Day' languished, Buddy Holly, to his chagrin, achieved his first success as a songwriter. Impressed by 'Words of Love', Peer–Southern, as was their right as publishers of the song, offered it to other artists to record, and it was picked up by a Canadian group, the Diamonds, who had just had a number two hit with 'Little Darlin''. They released 'Words of Love' as a single on 20 May and reached number thirteen on the pop charts in June (uniquely, Buddy's name is spelt 'Holley' on the writer's credit on this record). Buddy's far superior original version wasn't released until 20 June, with 'Mailman, Bring Me No More Blues' as the B-side, by which time the Diamonds had stolen his thunder and it was too late. Amazingly, Buddy's 'Words of Love' was never issued as a single in the UK at the time, although it did make a big impression on some musicians in Liverpool who later recorded it for one of their albums.

On 29 May, two days after the release of 'That'll Be The Day', the Crickets were back in Clovis recording some more tracks – 'Not Fade Away', 'Everyday', 'Ready Teddy', 'Valley of Tears', and 'Tell Me How'. No distinction was made at the time between the songs that would be released under the Crickets' name and those that would be released under Buddy Holly's name, but in most cases when the time did come to decide, vocal backings by the Picks were added to the Crickets releases, but not to the Buddy Holly releases. Niki Sullivan actually played only on 'Valley of Tears' and 'Tell Me How'. Because of Buddy's versatility, Niki wasn't really needed on records, and even when he did play in the studio he wasn't always miked up. Sullivan knew this made sense. As he told John Beecher, 'it's all on one track, and if I make a mistake, then we blow the whole thing.' But he was happy just being at the sessions: 'What else can you do in Clovis, New Mexico, at 2 o'clock in the morning?'

On 'Everyday', Buddy played acoustic guitar, Norman Petty played celeste, while J.I.'s 'drumming' simply consisted of a rhythm slapped out on his thighs; on 'Not Fade Away', he played a cardboard box (at one point hitting a cymbal by accident). The 'bop bop' backing vocals on this occasion were provided by Niki and overdubbed Buddy. On 'Valley of Tears', with Buddy's reluctant acquiescence, Petty joined the full Crickets line-up on organ, an instrument Buddy felt belonged in church.

The songwriting credits were by now being applied almost at random, but with Petty's name appearing on most. According to Petty, it didn't much matter what names appeared, as the band would be sharing the money out among themselves once it began coming in. So, for example, 'Not Fade Away', which started out as a Jerry Allison improvisation on the Bo Diddley beat, became credited to

Hardin–Petty – 'Charles Hardin' being the name Holly used for a time to disguise his songwriting activities from Cedarwood, before the conflict concerning the Nashville contract was resolved. In fact, Buddy Holly was clearly the songwriting force of the team, but happy to give credits, and royalties, to the other band members for suggesting odd lines or improvements.

A month later, at the end of June and with still no chart action, the Crickets returned to Clovis for what turned out to be their definitive recording session. Between 29 June and 1 July 1957 they recorded 'Peggy Sue', 'Listen to Me', 'Oh Boy!' and 'I'm Gonna Love You Too'. By chance, 'I'm Gonna Love You Too' includes the sound of a real cricket, which had got into the echo chamber and chirped exactly on the beat on the fade-out to the song. Niki Sullivan didn't actually play on any of these tracks, although he did make a crucial contribution to what became Buddy Holly's signature song, 'Peggy Sue'.

'Peggy Sue' started life as a Buddy Holly composition called 'Cindy Lou'. He got the name from his sister and his niece; Pat Holley, whose middle name was Lou (short for Louise), had a daughter called Cindy Carol Weir. All the members of Buddy's immediate family agree that that was the origin of the title. In its original incarnation, as featured in live performances, the song was slower, and had a Latin beat. But while the band were warming up in the Clovis studio, J.I. thrashed out a rolling rhythm, known as a paradiddle, often used as an exercise by drummers. He got the idea from the percussion on a song called 'Dawn', by Jaye P. Morgan, the B-side of 'That's All I Want From You'. Buddy liked the effect so much that he immediately suggested using it on 'Cindy Lou'.

This was easier said than done. For a start, the drumming was so loud that Norman Petty had to get J.I. to set up his kit in the reception area outside the studio. Secondly, it was extremely difficult, even for a drummer of J.I.'s capability, to maintain a steady rhythm of paradiddles throughout the recording. But Buddy hit on an incentive for his drummer.

Back in the summer of 1956, J.I. had split up with his high school girlfriend, Peggy Sue Gerron. Buddy knew Peggy Sue well; he and Echo had gone on double dates with Jerry and Peggy Sue, and since Echo's religious beliefs prevented her from dancing, Buddy had often danced with Peggy Sue. Because her mother had health problems, in 1957 Peggy Sue was living with her elder sister and brother-in-law in Sacramento, California. Still only in her mid-teens

(J.I. was not quite eighteen in July 1957), she was going to school there, but spending holidays with her parents in Lubbock. J.I. was eager to get back together with her, and had been pestering Buddy to use her name in a song that he could impress her with. So now, Buddy said he'd change the song to 'Peggy Sue' if J.I. could keep up the paradiddles all the way through. After one failure, Buddy threatened to change the song back to 'Cindy Lou' if he didn't get it right next time; but he did.

As J.I. rose to the task, Norman Petty made his most significant contribution to any Holly recording, flipping the control switch of the echo chamber repeatedly on and off so that the drumming became a rolling beat, coming and going like waves on a beach.

There was one last refinement to complete the sound. In order to change the guitar sound on the recording for the instrumental break, a switch had to be flipped on Buddy's Stratocaster at the crucial moment. He couldn't do this and play at the same time, so Niki Sullivan knelt in front of him to make the necessary adjustment. It was his only contribution to the recording. In all honesty, Joe B. might just as well have not been there either; but the end product was the definitive record of the rock 'n' roll era.

In order to allow J.I. to impress the real Peggy Sue, Buddy gave him the songwriting credit on the record. For his own reasons, Norman Petty added his name. 'Oh Boy!' had been written by Sonny West and Bill Tilghman, who had sent a demo to Petty and didn't even know that it was being recorded by Buddy; that didn't stop Petty adding his name as co-writer on that song as well, even though the most cursory listen to Sonny West's own version shows that Petty contributed nothing at all. On the other hand, comparison of West's version and Holly's version highlights the way Buddy could take someone else's song and make it his own with a vastly superior rendition; it wouldn't be the last time. By contrast, nobody, not even the Beatles, ever took a Buddy Holly song and improved upon his own recording of it.

At this stage, nobody had any idea what name the recordings would be released under, if they ever got released at all. One pair of demos sent to New York for consideration had 'Peggy Sue' and 'Oh Boy!' coupled under the name the Crickets, with 'Everyday' and 'Not Fade Away' labelled as by Buddy Holly. When the songs were eventually released, 'Peggy Sue'/'Everyday' had Holly's name on the record, while 'Oh Boy!'/'Not Fade Away' became

Crickets songs. But that wouldn't be until 'That'll Be The Day' eventually hit the charts.

During the sessions that produced 'Peggy Sue', news had come from New York that 'That'll Be The Day' had, almost surreptitiously, sold 50,000 copies. That was not enough to make it a national hit, but enough to persuade Brunswick to start promoting the record properly, and to buy the rights to 'Peggy Sue'/'Everyday' for an advance of $600. By then, the Crickets had even flown up to New York, at Decca's expense, to meet Bob Thiele and Murray Deutch, and to make a personal appearance at a Manhattan record store.

During the hot July of 1957, while sales of 'That'll Be The Day' slowly increased, Buddy, J.I. and Joe B. recorded two non-original songs, 'Send Me Some Loving' and 'It's Too Late', the latter at the special request of Buddy's brother Larry. Buddy also played on several sessions including one for the Norman Petty Trio, a Petty composition called 'Moondreams', and, increasingly frustrated by the long-distance romance with the chaste Echo McGuire, had a passionate affair with a married woman seven or eight years older than him, June Clark. The most significant event, though, was the Crickets' first booking for an East Coast tour, on the back of the growing interest in 'That'll Be The Day'. They were contracted to play in a package opening in Washington, DC, on 2 August before moving on to Baltimore and finishing with a seven-day stint at the Apollo Theatre in Harlem, New York.

The booking was due to a mistake on the part of the promoters. Unknown to the Lubbock boys, there was a black vocal group called the Crickets (who had actually disbanded by 1957), and the promoters of the all-black tour had assumed from the earthy sound of 'That'll Be The Day' that this was the group they were booking. Adding to the confusion, a black group called the Ravens had released a cover version of 'That'll Be The Day', and were getting some airplay.

Buddy, J.I, Niki and Joe B. realised a mistake had been made, since their fellow artists included Clyde McPhatter, Otis Rush, and other well-known black performers; the venues they were booked in to were also a dead giveaway, in the black ghettos where decent white folk never ventured. But Buddy and the Crickets had never encountered any hostility from the black performers they'd met, such as Little Richard, and Buddy was never in any doubt about his ability to please any audience. They signed anyway. That wasn't the only thing they agreed to. It was about this time that Norman Petty suggested that they needed a manager. They told him that they already had a manager – Norman Petty. J.I. told John Goldrosen how it happened:

> We all agreed that Norman *ought* to be the manager … anything we wanted to do [musically], he was willing to try it. Anyway, at the time, all we wanted to do was play rock 'n' roll music. We didn't want to hear about all the trivials, because we thought everything was straight ahead …

They were neither the first, nor the last, musicians to make that mistake. A bank account was opened 'for the band' on 24 July 1957, with a deposit of $500 (probably the money Buddy had asked Murray Deutch for). The cheques on the account were signed by Norman Petty; the first, on 25 July, was for $175, as a payment on Buddy's latest car.

In Washington and Baltimore, as Buddy had anticipated, the black audiences were won over as soon as the Crickets started playing and the audience had got over their bemusement at seeing four white boys up on the stage. It helped that on 12 August 'That'll Be The Day' at last entered the *Billboard* Top 100 (which would be renamed the 'Hot

100' in August 1958) at number 65. Even when Buddy was struck by laryngitis and Niki Sullivan had to sing lead for a couple of nights, the audience response was still good. When Norman Petty heard this, he is reported to have said: 'Well, anyone can sing those songs.' This is usually interpreted as a disparaging comment. I believe it was just the opposite. Whatever Norman Petty was, he was no fool when it came to music and no fool when it came to money. He was well aware that Buddy deliberately wrote songs that kids in high school bands could play. And if you think that's so easy, try it! The more the songs got played at hops, the more people would buy the records and the more people would know who Buddy Holly was. Sure, anyone could play the songs – but nobody could play them like Buddy Holly.

Even so, and contrary to legend, the Harlem audiences weren't so easily won over – and, also contrary to legend, by the time the tour reached New York the theatre management at the Apollo were well aware that the Crickets were white. For the first two nights, the band died on stage. 'That'll Be The Day' got a lukewarm response, but their other original songs went down like lead balloons. On the third evening, after their opening number drew no response, Buddy turned to the band and said: 'The heck with

it. Let's give 'em "Bo Diddley".' With the boys jump-
ing around like lunatics and 'working their butts
off', the song was greeted with rapturous applause.
'People just went bananas', Niki told John Beecher.
'From then on, we were accepted at the Apollo',
playing the kind of music Buddy loved and the audience wanted.

There was no time to rest on their laurels. At the
end of the Apollo engagement, on 23 August the
Crickets went to Philadelphia to appear on a major
TV show, *American Bandstand*. The same day they
learned that sales of 'That'll Be The Day' had topped
half a million. From there, it was back to New York to
appear in Alan Freed's package show *Holiday of Stars*
at the Brooklyn Paramount theatre.

Freed is a legendary figure in pop music history,
claiming to have invented the term 'rock 'n' roll' and
graduating from being a DJ to promoting musical
extravaganzas like this. The packages were made up
from many artists who each had time to do only one
or two songs, the hits coming one after another – a
little like a live juke box. The hits came from (in this
case) Little Richard, Larry Williams, the Del Vikings,
the Cleftones, Mickey and Sylvia, the Moonglows,
the Five Keys, King Curtis, the Crickets, and the
Alan Freed Orchestra backing up any singers who

didn't have their own band. With five or more shows a day this was a nice little earner for the promoter, and not too bad for the performers. For what their contract specified as 'a minimum of 29 shows a week', the Crickets split $1,100 between them.

The Crickets finished the Freed show on 8 September, the day after Buddy's 21st birthday, and the next day joined *The Biggest Show of Stars for 1957*, a touring package put together by Irving Feld for the General Artists Corporation (GAC). This was really the big time. The show included Chuck Berry, Fats Domino, Paul Anka, the Drifters, the Everly Brothers, Frankie Lymon and the Teenagers, LaVern Baker, Buddy Knox, Jimmie Bowen, the Spaniels, and the Bobettes. The tour had started on 6 September, but the Crickets joined it on 9 September, and stayed with it, criss-crossing the States and over the border into Canada, until late November. Travelling on tour buses, the performers made many new friends; the Crickets were shown the ropes by the Everlys, then about six months ahead of the Crickets in terms of chart success.

While the Crickets were on the road, on 23 September 'That'll Be The Day' at last made it to number one on the pop sales chart, replacing Paul Anka's 'Diana', and reached number two on the R&B singles chart. It was the best-selling single in the USA. But in those days, the *Billboard* Top 100 was based on a combination of actual sales and the number of times a record was played on the radio, so there 'That'll Be The Day' peaked at number three, proving only that the DJs weren't quite in tune with the record-buying public. In Britain, where the charts were based on sales alone, 'That'll Be The Day' moved much faster. Released on 10 September, it was number one by the first week in November, stayed there for three weeks, and sold an astonishing 431,000 copies in a country with a population so much smaller than that of the USA that selling 250,000 there was rarer than selling a million in America. The urgent problem for the Crickets, even before the *Show of Stars* tour ended, was the perennial one for any successful artist – 'follow that'.

Buddy Holly at Bradley's Barn Studio in Nashville, 26 January 1956, during his unsuccessful time with Decca.

The Crickets perform on the Ed Sullivan Show, New York, 1 December 1957. Left to right: Niki Sullivan, Buddy Holly, J.I. Allison and Joe B. Mauldin.

The Crickets rehearsing in Lubbock after the departure of Niki Sullivan.

A rare picture of Buddy without glasses.

Buddy and J.I. on stage. The core of the Crickets' sound.

The definitive Crickets line-up – Buddy, J.I. and Joe B.

The Trocadero cinema in south London where Buddy's British tour began on 1 March 1958.

Buddy on stage at the London Palladium, 2 March 1958.

CHAPTER FOUR

Rave On!

In a sense, the follow-up to 'That'll Be The Day' had already been released before 'That'll Be The Day' reached the top of the charts. 'Peggy Sue', coupled with 'Everyday', came out under Buddy Holly's name on 20 September 1957, and was an integral part of the Crickets' act on the *Show of Stars*. *Cash Box* described it as a 'hot two-sider that could establish Buddy Holly as a name to be reckoned with'. The nearest equivalent would have been if 'From Me To You', the follow-up to the Beatles' 'Please Please Me', had been released under the name John Lennon – after all, he wrote both of the songs, and sang lead on both records. The big difference between the Crickets and the Beatles, though, was that John Lennon had an equal songwriting partner; even Paul McCartney's solo classic 'Yesterday' was issued under the group's name.

Peggy Sue Gerron tells how the *Show of Stars* came to Sacramento on 18 October, and how strange it was to see the name 'Buddy Holly and the Crickets', with no 'e' in 'Holly', on the advertisements, along with the names of many performers whose records she owned, now including Eddie Cochran, who had joined the tour. Cochran and Holly became close friends, described by several people who knew them as 'like brothers'. 'Everybody knew that being with the *Show of Stars* meant you'd *made* it', says Peggy Sue. 'Buddy Holly and the Crickets' was, incidentally, increasingly the way the group were billed, and the way the name appeared on J.I.'s bass drum, even before 'Peggy Sue' was released.

Before arriving in Sacramento, Jerry Allison (belying the image of rock drummers of later years!) got his mother to phone Peggy Sue's mother to obtain permission to invite Peggy Sue to the show, promising her a special surprise. As far as she recalls, she hadn't yet heard the Crickets' records, because she didn't listen to the radio and her own collection consisted almost entirely of records by black R&B artists. So it came as a complete surprise when at the end of the short set Buddy stepped up to the mike and quietened the audience down before announcing, 'This is a special show tonight, and we're playing this song for a special person', before launching into 'Peggy Sue'.

Even though the attention of the audience was focused on the stage, 'I suddenly felt the whole world was looking at me. At seventeen, my sole objective in social situations was to keep from being noticed. I was so embarrassed I could have died.' She managed to get over it, and making her way backstage with Jerry during an intermission after the set was greeted by Buddy with the words: 'Aren't you glad your mother named you after my new hit song?' The favour to J.I. had worked its magic, and he was back together with Peggy Sue, who Buddy took to calling 'Song'.

'Peggy Sue' was indeed high in the charts in October 1957, reaching number three on the pop sales chart and number two on the R&B chart and selling well over a million copies. In the UK, it reached number six. Cashing in on Buddy's success, since August Decca had been releasing singles from his Nashville sessions, starting with the inferior version of 'That'll Be The Day', coupled with 'Rock Around With Ollie Vee', and eventually including an album also titled *That'll Be The Day*. There was nothing Buddy could do but wait for the supply to dry up.

For the second Crickets single, Norman Petty took

the recording of 'Oh Boy!' made at the same sessions that had produced 'Peggy Sue', and added vocal backings from the Picks, somewhat in the spirit of the vocal backings on 'That'll Be The Day', to distinguish it from a Buddy Holly solo release. It sounds better without them. Coupled with a similarly doctored 'Not Fade Away' ('Not Fade Away' was merely a Holly B-side!), it came out on 27 October and reached number ten in the pop sales chart, a surprisingly low thirteen on the R&B chart, but a more impressive number three in the UK. 'That'll Be The Day', 'Peggy Sue' and 'Oh Boy!' were the only American top ten hits Buddy Holly ever had, and they were all released before the end of 1957. Britain was (and remains) consistently more enthusiastic, although curiously the only Buddy Holly record that got higher in the US chart than in the UK was 'Peggy Sue'.

With two hits in the higher reaches of the chart and 'That'll Be The Day' still selling well, Buddy Holly and the Crickets needed to put an album (then simply called a long player, or LP) out quickly. The stockpile of Clovis material didn't quite provide enough in the way of suitable masters, bearing in mind the need to maintain Buddy's solo career as well, and with the Crickets on the road Petty found an ingenious solution to the problem.

For a week at the end of September 1957, while the *Show of Stars* travelled through southern states where white and black performers were not allowed to appear on stage together, the white artists on the bill had some time off. The snag was, the Norman Petty Trio was also on the road. So after a flying visit home to Lubbock, the Crickets rendezvoused with Petty at Tinker Air Force Base, near Oklahoma City, where he had set up his recording equipment, including the Ampex machine, in the officers' club. On 29 September they recorded four new tracks: Roy Orbison's songs 'An Empty Cup' and 'You've Got Love', 'Rock Me My Baby', and a new version of 'Maybe Baby'. All were overdubbed with vocals by the Picks when Petty got back to Clovis.

The idea for the more 'rock' version of 'Maybe Baby' came, indirectly, from Little Richard. On the tour, the Crickets had been playing the song with what J.I. calls 'a swing beat' (*Memories*). The singer Dale Hawkins (a cousin of Ronnie Hawkins) heard the song and 'said, "Hey, why don't you do it with the same beat as 'Lucille'," which was one of Little Richard's big hits on the show.' So they did. The result was so good that it was released as a Crickets single in February 1958, coupled with 'Tell Me How'. It only reached number seventeen on the US pop chart, but number four on the R&B chart and also number four in the UK.

The LP, called *The Chirpin' Crickets*, came out on 27 November 1957, three days after the *Show of Stars* tour ended in Richmond, Virginia (later copies restored the 'g' to 'Chirping'). The tracks on it were: 'Oh Boy!', 'Not Fade Away', 'You've Got Love', 'Maybe Baby', It's Too Late', 'Tell Me How', 'That'll Be The Day', 'I'm Lookin' For Someone To Love', 'An Empty Cup', 'Send Me Some Lovin'', 'Last Night', and 'Rock Me My Baby'. Many of the songs suffer from the heavy-handed overdubbing of the Picks' vocals, done by Petty while the Crickets were on the road. Four days later, on 1 December, the Crickets appeared on the *Ed Sullivan Show*, performing 'That'll Be The Day' and 'Peggy Sue' live. Niki Sullivan's guitar wasn't plugged in for the performance. Ed Sullivan, who was no fan of rock 'n' roll, was to some extent won over by Holly's natural courtesy and good manners in a short on-camera interview, but was clearly unimpressed by the music. The album never made the charts in the US, but reached number five in the UK.

On 4 December Buddy and the boys at last got back to Lubbock, which they hadn't seen – apart from the flying visit in late September – for four months, since the beginning of August. The city took no notice at all of the return of the biggest stars – indeed, the most famous people – Lubbock had ever produced; as far as the general population was concerned, the boys might have just got back from a tiling job.

Niki Sullivan promptly announced that he was leaving the band, complaining that he was exhausted and hated touring. This was only half the story. Niki and J.I. hadn't been getting along too well, and had occasionally even come to blows when J.I.'s horseplay got out of hand. Buddy and J.I. were long-time friends, and Joe B. was happy to play along with J.I.'s antics, so Niki was increasingly isolated. It didn't help that he was well aware that he was contributing nothing musically.

The attitude of the other Crickets was, well, if he wants to quit, OK; no hard feelings. There was some talk of asking Sonny Curtis back into the band, but by now Sonny had his own career going, and in any case Buddy and J.I. scarcely even needed a bass player, let alone another guitarist. They decided to carry on as a trio. Niki tried and failed to make a career in music as a solo artist, and ended up working for Sony; he died unexpectedly, of a heart attack, in 2004 at the age of 66. He had shown no signs of ill-health, and completed a round of golf earlier that same day.

In early 1958, his most pressing problem was getting the quarter share of the Crickets' earnings and the songwriting royalties that he was entitled to. Norman Petty had all the band's money under his control, but proved so evasive that in the end Niki settled for $1,000. Adding insult to injury, his church never received the promised tithe – indeed, none of the Crickets' churches ever received their 40 per cents. Years later, Niki told Philip Norman: 'My dad was right in what he said the first time he ever met Norman [Petty]. "Son, NEVER trust a businessman who keeps a Bible on his desk."'

Buddy, J.I. and Joe B. had a few days' rest before they had to get back to work. Buddy took the opportunity to have his hair styled – he always had difficulty keeping his naturally curly hair in order – and his front teeth capped, at a cost of $596 (twice the cost of a Strat!). The bills, like all his bills, were paid for by Petty out of the band account, and occasional sums of cash were drawn for the Crickets, but getting significant amounts of money out of Norman, as Niki was discovering, was next to impossible. Eager to keep the flow of funds going in his direction, as well as signing a few cheques, around this time Petty also signed the Crickets up to three more commitments – an Alan Freed Christmas show in New York (another

Holiday of Stars), a package tour with *America's Great-est Teenage Recording Stars*, and a short tour of Florida. Before leaving for New York, between 17 and 19 December the trio were back recording in Clovis, with the prospect of a 'solo' Buddy Holly LP in mind.

The numbers they laid down were 'Little Baby' (credited to Holly–Petty–Kendall), 'You're So Square (Baby I Don't Care)' (a Leiber–Stoller composition made famous by Elvis), and 'Look at Me' (Holly–Petty–Allison). C.W. Kendall Jr, the co-composer of 'Little Baby', played piano on that song, while on 'Look at Me' Vi played piano, and on 'You're So Square' J.I., again borrowing a trick from the Rhythm Orchids, played a cardboard box. This is one of the definitive Holly–Allison musical collabo-rations. It was also during these sessions that Buddy and J.I., rehearsing in the studio, taped their tantalis-ingly incomplete versions of 'Mona'.

The day after the sessions, Buddy picked up a brand-new car, a pink two-seater Impala V-8. But he scarcely had time to enjoy it before he was leaving Lubbock again. He may not have been too sorry to leave, since it was on this pre-Christmas visit home in 1957 that he learned that Echo McGuire had fallen for someone else; she married Ron Griffith on St Valentine's Day in 1958.

Back in New York from 23 December 1957 to 5 January 1958, for the Freed shows 'Buddy Holly' and 'the Crickets' were, for the first time anywhere, billed as separate attractions – even though it was the same band with the same singer! For less than two weeks' work, they were paid $4,200 – but on 28 December they were paid nearly half that, $2,000, for a single appearance playing a single song, 'Peggy Sue', on the *Arthur Murray* TV show. On stage, Buddy and the Crickets were the big hits of the show, often getting two or three encores, where the other artists got none. Off stage, the disappointment at being away from home for Christmas was compensated for by their fellow stars the Everly Brothers, who continued their education of the country boys into the delights of the big city, including dining in good restaurants, buying smart clothes, and even (according to Don and Phil themselves) suggesting the most important change to Buddy's image. If you're going to wear glasses, they told him, wear ones that make a statement – don't try to hide the fact. Jerry Allison remembers giving him the same advice.

There was scarcely time for the Crickets to catch their breath after the Freed show before the *Teenage Stars* tour, which ran from 8 January to 24 January. Before that tour even started, Petty had signed them to join Paul Anka and Jerry Lee Lewis on a tour of Australia, with a stopover in Hawaii, starting on 27 January. But that just left time between tours to make Holly's first recordings in New York, on 25 January 1958, at the Bell Sound Studios. The idea was Buddy's, and the session was set up for him by Bob Thiele. Petty, anxious that Buddy was starting to branch out on his own, was present at the session; as a sop, he was allowed to play piano.

The reason why Buddy was so keen to squeeze in the session was that Sonny West and Bill Tilghman had come up with an even better song than 'Oh Boy!'. The song was 'Rave On'. What more is there to say? If you don't understand that comment, all I *can* say is, listen to the record! The same session also produced a version of the standard 'That's My Desire', which by Buddy's standards was just a filler. Buddy didn't play guitar on either track, concentrating on his singing. The musicians were J.I. and Joe B., Norman Petty, guitarist Al Caiola, rhythm guitarist Donald Arnone, and backing vocals from the Jivetones. It is easy to imagine the trepidation that Norman Petty must have felt at this proof that Buddy Holly didn't need him, or his studio, to produce great records.

The Crickets' last commitment before leaving New York was a second appearance on the *Ed Sullivan*

Show. This was pretty much a disaster. Sullivan objected to their choice of 'Oh Boy!' as their song, even though it was their current hit, as he found the lyrics suggestive. As the show was live, Buddy played it anyway, but Sullivan childishly ordered the sound to be turned down and the lights dimmed by the engineers. Buddy never played on the *Ed Sullivan Show* again (surprisingly, he was asked back, but turned them down, commenting that they didn't have enough money to make it worth his time). But the show is memorable visually for the first appearance of Buddy's new glasses, the famous black horn-rims, purchased in New York a few days before.

Norman Petty accompanied the Crickets on their trip to Hawaii and Australia, behaving more like a tourist than a manager, but travelling, of course, at the band's expense. If there was ever any real business to conduct, such as sorting out the billing on the shows, it was Buddy who did the negotiating. In fact, at a time when artists such as Jerry Lee Lewis, who had just had a huge hit with 'Great Balls of Fire' and was about to reach the top with 'Breathless', were insisting on top billing, Buddy was more laid-back, and would accept a lower spot on the bill in exchange for a larger fee. He knew his set would be great, whenever he played it; and since 'That'll Be

The Day', 'Peggy Sue', and 'Oh Boy!' had each reached number two in the Australian charts, everybody knew who the biggest stars of the show were, whatever the order of names or size of print on the posters.

Petty's involvement was – well, more petty. It was felt at the time that if a recording star got married, his career would suffer because he would lose his appeal to single girls. Even five years later, John Lennon was advised to keep his marriage secret for this reason. So when J.I. announced that he intended to marry Peggy Sue, Norman suggested to Buddy that they should fire J.I. and get another drummer. Buddy retorted that since Norman was already married, perhaps they should fire *him*, and get another manager.

The stopover in Honolulu, necessary because the airliners of the day didn't have the range to reach Australia in one hop, provided the opportunity for a little sightseeing and two sell-out concerts. The short Australian tour, which took in Sydney, Melbourne, Brisbane and Newcastle, was equally successful, in more ways than one. It cemented a friendship between Buddy and Paul Anka, anther prolific songwriter, and it introduced the Crickets to possibly the only genuine Australian rock 'n' roll performer,

Johnny O'Keefe, who played on the package and was best known for his big Australian hit, 'Wild One'. On 10 February, the Crickets arrived home, also via Honolulu where they did another show, with just time to lay down a few tracks in Clovis before heading off to Florida on 20 February for a five-day tour with Jerry Lee Lewis, Bill Haley (remember him?), the Everly Brothers and the Royal Teens (who? You may well ask! Their best-selling record was a novelty number called 'Short Shorts', which became a feature of the stage act of Freddie and the Dreamers. Their pianist, Bob Gaudio, later became a member of the Four Seasons). While they had been in Australia, Buddy's single coupling 'Listen to Me' with 'I'm Gonna Love You Too' had been released on 5 February. Neither side charted in the US, but 'Listen to Me' reached number sixteen in the UK. 'Maybe Baby' was released a week later. The lack of success of the records in the US may indicate that the cunning plan of making almost simultaneous releases by the same artist under two names was no longer such a good idea.

Whatever the charts said, though, Buddy Holly's powers were in no way waning. The tracks recorded between 12 February and 19 February were of the highest class. One of my personal favourites, 'Well

... All Right', features Buddy on vocal and acoustic guitar, Joe B. on bass, and J. I. tapping the rhythm on cymbal alone. Its composition was credited to all three Crickets, plus Norman Petty, but it's doubtful anyone contributed much except Buddy, who got the idea for the title from an expression Little Richard used to holler out on stage. Petty did make a significant contribution to the sound, though, by placing a microphone *inside* Buddy's guitar. 'Take Your Time' (a Holly–Petty song to which Petty made a definite contribution of at least one line, the one about heartstrings singing like a ball of twine) included Petty on organ, and another of Holly's best recordings, 'Fool's Paradise', used just the standard Crickets line-up. It was written by Sonny LeGlare and Horace Linsley, although Norman Petty's name appeared on this one as well. The last Crickets song to be recorded at this time was 'Think It Over', credited to Holly–Petty–Allison. From now on, where Petty deemed it appropriate, vocal backings were dubbed on later not by the Picks, but by a group called the Roses.

At the end of these sessions, two more songs were recorded with J. I. singing lead and Bo Clarke playing drums. The first was his version of 'Wild One', retitled 'Real Wild Child'. The second was a jokey version of 'Oh, You Beautiful Doll', just to fill up the

B-side of a single. They were released under the name Ivan (J.I.'s middle name) and reached number 68 on the pop chart. As Jerry put it in a later interview (*The Definitive Story*), 'it started at the bottom of the charts and worked its way across.'

The Florida tour followed immediately after the recording sessions, from 20 February to 25 February. When the Everlys, who didn't have their own backing band, were provided with incompetent amateurs to support them, Buddy and the Crickets volunteered to step into the breach, appearing behind their friends as well as in their own set. The Everlys had the tricky task of following Jerry Lee Lewis on stage. 'Only by the grace of God and Buddy Holly and the Crickets did Don and I manage to pull it off' (Phil Everly, *The Real Buddy Holly Story*); 'when Buddy Holly came back and played for us, it was just pandemonium.'

Somewhere on the tour, possibly after the last show, in Fort Lauderdale on 25 February, a jam session involving some of the stars was recorded on tape; a snippet survives of Buddy singing part of the song 'Drown In My Own Tears', with Jerry Lee Lewis on piano. The same week, Coral released Buddy's 'solo' LP, simply titled *Buddy Holly*. Like the *Chirping Crickets* LP, it didn't make the album charts in the

US, but fared better in the UK, where it went to number eight. The tracks on it were 'I'm Gonna Love You Too', 'Peggy Sue', 'Look At Me', 'Listen To Me', 'Valley of Tears', 'Ready Teddy', 'Everyday', 'Mailman, Bring Me No More Blues', 'Words of Love', 'You're So Square', 'Rave On', and 'Little Baby'.

Still there was no rest for the Crickets. On 27 February they set off on an overnight flight to London, with tourists Norman and Vi tagging along. They were about to begin the most significant and influential tour in the entire history of popular music, which would inspire the musicians who shortly became the Beatles, the Rolling Stones, the Searchers, and many lesser lights such as Freddie and the Dreamers, who took Buddy's music, tweaked it a little, and in a few years came roaring back with it across the Atlantic to lay by its ears an America that had never fully appreciated its home-grown genius. The 'British Beat Boom of the Sixties' began on Saturday, 1 March 1958, when Buddy Holly and the Crickets played the Trocadero cinema at London's Elephant and Castle, and took off the following day when they appeared at the Gaumont in Kilburn and on the top British TV show of its day, *Sunday Night at the London Palladium*. That TV appearance gave budding guitarists such as George Harrison, Eric Clapton and Keith Richards their first chance to even see a Fender Stratocaster, while John Lennon and Paul McCartney were among the musicians with noses pressed up against the TV screens trying to work out the chords Buddy was playing.

A superb account of the British tour is provided by Philip Norman, who was sixteen when Buddy died and grew up to become the best of rock biographers. Ellis Amburn's version is worth reading for its unintentionally hilarious vision of a mythical parallel-reality Britain, perhaps based on viewing too many bad Hollywood movies, suffocated by 'an antiquated and repressive caste system', with London full of 'immaculate white town houses', the BBC 'the only TV and radio network' (*Sunday Night at the London Palladium* was actually on the rival ITV), and many more. Amburn also seems to be under the delusion that Australia is part of the United Kingdom. If this is any guide, it's small wonder that some people who knew Buddy describe the Amburn book as containing elements of fiction.

Instead of trying to cover the same ground as Philip Norman, I'll content myself with offering one representative review from the tour, and one anecdote about Buddy Holly. After their performance in Birmingham, the review read:

Buddy Holly, leader of the group, is a studious-looking young man who totes his electric guitar like a sawn-off shot-gun and carries around a giant-sized amplifier which even made the Town Hall organ pipes flinch. Mr Holly is 70 per cent of the act. He plays and sings with brash exuberance, and adds a few Presley-like wiggles which had the teenage audience squealing with delight. The rest of the group consists of a bass player whose ability was lost in the noise and a drummer who plays with sledge-hammer precision.

At every gig, among the thousands of squealing girls there were dozens of teenage boys looking on in wonder and thinking: 'I could do that. I *want* to do that!' On 14 March, one of those kids at the Woolwich Granada was fourteen-year-old Mick Jagger, attending his first-ever rock 'n' roll show, and hearing 'Not Fade Away' for the first time anywhere. The 'giant-sized' amplifier (a 50-watt Fender Bassman, with four ten-inch speakers, designed for electric bass but much favoured by guitarists of the day) would seem pathetically small by modern standards, but one of the wonders of the British tour for those boys was how Buddy and J.I. managed to play so loud (Joe B., as the review suggests, couldn't be heard at all more than a couple of rows back from the stage). The other wonder was that the Crickets sounded exactly the same on stage as they did on record. This was literally unheard of.

In order to appreciate the Buddy Holly story, you need to know what kind of British package tour the Crickets were on. This wasn't a *Show of Teenage Recording Stars* like the American package tours, but a variety show including an orchestra playing Glenn Miller-type music, ballad singers, and even a juggling act. Buddy and the Crickets were the only rock 'n' roll act, top of the bill, and the group everyone wanted to see, but first the audience had to sit through all the rest. The compere of the show, introducing the acts, was a young comedian called Des O'Connor.

He recalls: 'We were touring with the Ronnie Keene Orchestra, which had 28 musicians with a front line of 16 brass, then out come the Crickets, just three of them, and I couldn't make out how they were making ten times as much noise. It was so exciting and vibrant and I knew that something exciting was happening.' (*Memories*)

Buddy used to watch the comedian's act from the wings, fascinated by his interaction with the audience, and got Des to teach him a few jokes, which he tried out between the Crickets' numbers. Getting a good response, he added more patter as the tour went on. Writing home on 22 March, he told his parents: 'Everyone commented on how my jokes get bigger laughs than the comedian on the show, Des O'Connor.' Des says that this is not surprising, since he had been using O'Connor's jokes, but delivering them 'in a real Southern drawl ... the audience loved his accent, and jokes that I wouldn't get laughs with would be downright funny when he delivered them' (*Memories*). In exchange, at the end of the tour Buddy gave Des an acoustic guitar he'd bought in England. Des never learned to play, but it's still one of his treasured possessions.

As an example of Buddy's stage banter, on this tour he used to introduce 'Rip It Up' like this:

Here's a sad little song with tender lyrics that really tell a story. This tune is likely to reduce you all to tears, not because of the sadness of the words, but on account of the pathetic way we sing it.

The audiences loved it.

The Crickets played their last show in London on 25 March 1958. As soon as they were back in the

States, they joined an exhausting 44-day tour as part of *Alan Freed's Big Beat Show*. Many old friends were on the tour, including Chuck Berry and Jerry Lee Lewis, but that didn't make it any less tiring. One thing that did make it less tiring was that on this well-organised tour many of the journeys between gigs were made by air – even if the planes involved were often rickety ex-World War Two DC3 Dakotas.

By now, Buddy, J.I. and Joe B. had realised that sending money back to Clovis as Norman Petty demanded (they were often paid, in cash, a share of the receipts at the shows) was equivalent, for all their chances of seeing it again, to throwing it out of the window of one of the DC3s. So Buddy took care of the finances. Sometimes he would share the money out on a 'one for you, one for me' basis, counting out each dollar bill with mock seriousness. More often, he would throw it in a heap on the bed of one of their hotel rooms, and the three of them would dive in to grab what they could. While they were on this tour, on 20 April Coral released 'Rave On'/'Take Your Time' as the latest Buddy Holly single. This was the first single under Buddy's solo name to feature backing vocals; since the Jivetones were recorded with Buddy at the same session, the feel is, ironically, more like 'That'll Be The Day' than any of the other

Crickets singles to date, with the backing vocals in the background where they belong, instead of being too intrusive as a result of being overdubbed later with too heavy a hand. One of the great records of the rock 'n' roll era, 'Rave On' reached a pathetic number 37 in the US pop chart, but soared to number five in the UK.

The tour ended early in May, a few days prematurely, after trouble broke out during a show in Boston and a Navy sailor was stabbed. This happened outside the arena where the show was on, but inside the arena there was also a disturbance caused by white youths who objected to black and white performers appearing on stage together. This became known as the 'Boston riot', and led to the cancellation of the last few legs of the tour by city authorities looking for an excuse to ban rock 'n' roll.

With money in their pockets and the first free time they had had in months, on the way home the trio stopped off in Dallas to buy motorcycles. They wanted Harley-Davidsons, but the sales staff at the Harley dealership didn't believe they had the money to pay for them, and treated them as timewasters. So the Crickets went across town to the Triumph dealership, where they and their money were welcomed with open arms. They bought an Ariel Cyclone for

Buddy, a Triumph Trophy for J. I., a Thunderbird for Joe B., and all the appropriate clothing carrying the Triumph emblem, for a total of around $3,000. Then they headed off for Lubbock, taking care to roar past the Harley dealership on the way.

With cash in hand, Buddy was also eager to repay his debts – the $1,000 he owed Larry, and, to their astonishment, twice what they had lent him, and long since written off, to all the friends who had supported him in the hard times.

On 25 May, after a short break relaxing, fooling around on their motorbikes and generally having a good time, the Crickets returned to Clovis for more recording sessions. There, they joined up with a guitarist called Tommy Allsup. Allsup, who was five years older than Buddy, was an established musician from Oklahoma, who had been doing session work in Clovis. His style, picking one string at a time, was a world away from Buddy Holly's 'rhythm lead', which involved playing chords across all six strings at once, as on the 'Peggy Sue' solo – this technique derived partly from Buddy's experience playing banjo. But Allsup was a brilliant guitarist who Holly immediately invited to join the recordings. Buddy didn't care about playing second fiddle – or second guitar – behind someone who could contribute something new and worthwhile to the Buddy Holly sound.

The first two tracks recorded with Allsup were 'Lonesome Tears' (Holly) and 'It's So Easy' (Holly–Petty), both featuring Buddy on vocal and acoustic guitar, Tommy Allsup on lead guitar, Joe B. on bass and J.I. on drums. Next came a beautiful Bob Montgomery song, 'Heartbeat', recorded using the same line-up except that Joe B. was replaced by a session musician, 37-year-old George Atwood. Norman (and, by his acquiescence, presumably Buddy as well) had got tired of trying to work around Joe B.'s mistakes. According to Atwood (*Memories*), he is also the uncredited bass player on some of the earlier Holly records; sometimes, he says, Norman Petty would record a new track by the Crickets twice, once with them all miked up and once with a board between Joe B. and the others, so that his bass couldn't be heard on the tape. 'If Joe B. got it wrong, I'd go in and add a bass to it.' 'Heartbeat' should have been a huge hit for Buddy; but the song had to wait until 1992 for Nick Berry to take an anaemic cover of it to number two in the UK, admittedly on the back of its use in the TV series of the same name.

In a clear sign of the way (one of the ways!) Buddy saw his career developing, the next session, a week later, didn't involve any other Crickets at all. With Bob Montgomery, Buddy had written two songs that he wanted to offer to his friends the Everly Brothers, and had no intention of releasing himself. With Buddy singing lead (and dual-tracking himself to produce an Everly Brothers-type sound) and playing acoustic guitar, Allsup on lead guitar, Atwood on bass and Bo Clarke on drums, he recorded 'Love's Made A Fool Of You' and 'Wishing'.

Ever the perfectionist, Holly didn't dash these off as mere demos, but produced (and by now he was the producer, even if it was Norman Petty's studio) complete, finished recordings of the highest standard. It is impossible to imagine anyone else who could have produced such perfect hit material and then offered it to someone else; nor is it easy to understand why, when the songs were eventually released, Petty found it necessary to add more instrumentation. Don and Phil were eager to record the songs, especially 'Wishing', but their management wouldn't allow this, because the songs weren't published by the people with whom they had a financial connection. They wanted the brothers to record only songs that would bring the management publishing income – preferably songs by husband-and-wife team Boudleaux and Felice Bryant, part of the same outfit. To soften the blow, the official reason given for the rejection was that the Holly versions were so good that the Everlys wouldn't be able to compete if Coral decided to issue them.

In the week between the recording of 'Heartbeat' and the session for the two Holly–Montgomery songs, Buddy received his formal request to report for a medical examination to see if he was fit for his statutory period of military service. His 20/800 eyesight and ulcer were more than enough to have him classified 4-F and leave him free to continue his career. But he was in no hurry. Apart from these sessions, which hardly counted as work, having been touring or recording almost continuously from the beginning of August 1957 until the beginning of May 1958, for the first time the Crickets had a few weeks to enjoy the fruits of their success. Even then, an offer of another tour came in, but Buddy turned it down flat. When J.I. suggested that they should grab the opportunity to make money while the offers were still coming in, he replied: 'What if you get killed tomorrow? And you didn't have any time to enjoy the money we've already made? What about that? If we just work all the time and don't enjoy ourselves? And I said, "You're right!" That was a whole new thought for me.' (J.I., *The Real Buddy Holly Story*). Allison remains grateful to this day that he took Buddy's advice, and his friend did indeed enjoy his holiday.

June 1958 gave the Crickets a rare opportunity to do some promotional work, flying to California, where among other things they visited Buddy's publishers, Southern Music, in Hollywood, and Buddy was interviewed on TV in San Francisco. On 18 June, J.I. and Joe B. flew back to Lubbock, but Buddy went to New York to carry out a solo recording session at the request of Dick Jacobs, who had recently taken over from Bob Thiele as head of A&R at Coral.

The background to the request was unusual. A young singer-songwriter called Bobby Darin had been making unsuccessful records on the Atco label, and was coming to the end of his contract. Fed up with Atco, he was planning to move to Brunswick, and had already recorded two songs for them, a great rocker called 'Early In The Morning' and the very inferior 'Now We're One', to be used as his first single for them, under the name the Ding Dongs. But just before his contract with Atco ran out, they released a novelty number by Darin called 'Splish Splash', whose lyric, incidentally, includes a reference to Peggy Sue and girls from other songs.

When 'Splish Splash' proved a surprise hit, Atco

renewed Darin's contract; when they learned about the Brunswick session, they demanded the tapes so that they could release 'Early In The Morning' themselves. Furious at losing both Darin and the song, Dick Jacobs got Buddy to record the same two songs, using the same producer (himself), the same arrangement, the same musicians, and the same backing singers, in the same location, the splendidly named Pythian Temple studio in New York. This recording, made on 19 June 1958, gives a whole new depth of meaning to the term 'cover version'. Rushed into the shops on 5 July, the single reached number 32 on what was by August, when the record charted, the Hot 100, and number seventeen in the UK. Darin's version got to number 24 on the Hot 100.

'Early In The Morning' was the first Buddy Holly record that I actually saw, since one of my uncles had a copy; he later passed it on to me, and I still have it. Apart from this personal connection, the significance of these events lies not so much in the record, although it's excellent, but the fact that Buddy was acting completely independently of the other Crickets or Norman Petty. 'Early In The Morning' was the first genuine Buddy Holly solo single.

Around this time, Buddy made another significant move away from his West Texas background and towards a future in New York; he decided to marry Maria Elena Santiago. As with the recording of 'Early In The Morning', though, the story is not quite what it seems at first sight.

The romantic version of the story, promoted by Maria Elena after Buddy's death, says that on some unspecified date in June 1958, Buddy, J.I. and Joe B. paid a visit to Murray Deutch at Peer–Southern in New York. Maria Elena, who was then 25 years old, was a Puerto Rican from a middle-class family who was living with her aunt, an executive who ran the Latin-American division at Peer–Southern. Because of this connection, she was filling in as a receptionist at Peer–Southern, where her Spanish came in useful. So she happened to be sitting at her desk outside the door to Deutch's inner office when the Crickets arrived. While waiting for Deutch to be free, the boys got to fooling around and flirting with her, and there was an instant spark between her and Buddy. Buddy begged her to go on a date that night, but even at the age of 25 Maria Elena was in the strict care of her aunt, Provi, who only reluctantly agreed after checking round the company with people like Murray Deutch to find out what kind of a young man Buddy was.

Over dinner, Buddy proposed. Maria Elena

thought he was kidding, but in the spirit of the game said he would need her aunt's permission – sure that he would never ask, and that if he did he would never get it. At nine o'clock the next morning, Buddy turned up at the apartment Maria Elena and Provi shared, and charmed the aunt, a strict, Catholic, Latin American lady, into agreeing. The rest, as they say, is history.

Only, it couldn't have happened quite like that. Over the years, after reading this story many times in different places, I'd always wondered why Buddy had never met Maria Elena on his previous visits to Peer–Southern. He could hardly have failed to notice a pretty, petite Puerto Rican girl sitting outside Murray Deutch's door! It was only when I was researching the material for this book that I learned about an interview Maria Elena gave to *16* magazine early in 1959, which gives an only slightly less romantic account of the only slightly less whirlwind romance that actually took place.

In that interview, Maria Elena says that the pair met 'early' in January 1958, which probably means before the *Teenage Recording Stars* tour. Since then, she had often seen Buddy around Peer–Southern, but at first only to say hello or nod a greeting in passing. The spark between them occurred when she was lunching with a friend at Howard Johnson's one day and the Crickets, accompanied by Norman Petty, turned up and were invited to join the girls. This would probably have been in late January 1958, around the time of the 'Rave On' session. It was after this meeting, according to the *16* interview, that Buddy turned to Petty and said: 'You see that girl? I'm going to marry her.'

The date of this remark explains why the later exchanges between Petty and Buddy about J.I.'s plans to get married were so heated. But it was 'months' later, probably around the time of the *Big Beat* tour, that Buddy and Maria Elena got closer together and shared a kiss in the back of a taxi. Maria Elena certainly attended one of the early performances of *Alan Freed's Big Beat Show* in New York in March, accompanied by Sonny Curtis. While Buddy was touring, they kept in touch by phone three or four times a day, and it was in June, around the time of the 'Early In The Morning' session, that they jointly sought and got Aunt Provi's approval of the marriage.

This account fits the dates when Buddy was in New York, allowing that nobody's memory is perfect. The romantic myth version of the story seems to have combined the events of January, March and late

June 1958 into one hectic couple of days. But whatever the details of the romance, what matters in personal terms is that Buddy and Maria Elena fell in love, and determined to get married in spite of the obvious problems of a white Baptist boy marrying a Catholic Latina girl. In professional terms, what matters is that Norman Petty rightly saw Maria Elena as a threat to his already-slipping grip on Buddy Holly, not least since her family connections would give her access to the true records of how much money he was siphoning off from the Crickets. He must have realised that Buddy would soon be gone, and he was right. But the momentum of the Crickets sustained the increasingly rocky professional relationship for another four months before the inevitable split.

CHAPTER FIVE

Gone

On 4 July 1958, the Crickets began a ten-day tour billed as the *Summer Dance Party*. The only other permanent artists on the tour, which was essentially a Buddy Holly showcase, were Tommy Allsup and his Western Swing Band. Tommy also played lead with the Crickets; local groups joined the bill at various gigs. The day after the tour began, 'Think It Over' was released as the Crickets' new single (the same day as 'Early In The Morning'!), with the even better 'Fool's Paradise' on the flip. In what was becoming a familiar story, 'Think It Over' reached number 27 on the Hot 100, but number eleven in the UK. Proving that the American record-buying public did have some sense, though, 'Fool's Paradise' charted in its own right, reaching number 58 on the Hot 100. Like so many of the Crickets' records, it sounds better still without the overdubbed 'backing' vocals.

With such a small touring party, there was no tour bus involved this time. The three Crickets travelled in Buddy's latest car, a blue Lincoln, while the four members of the Western Swing Band (including Tommy Allsup) officially travelled in a yellow DeSoto station wagon purchased with money from the Crickets' account, although Tommy often rode in the Lincoln. The DeSoto towed a small trailer loaded with all the equipment. The travelling was made easier because for this trip Joe B. had switched from upright bass to electric bass (a Stratocaster Precision model), which was much more convenient on the road; but at Buddy's insistence, he stuck with upright bass for the remainder of the recording sessions they did together, so as not to change the feel of the records. Without knowing it, Buddy and his band had now created the archetypal group line-up of the 1960s and beyond – two guitars, electric bass, and drums.

Buddy and Tommy also had new guitars for this tour. Buddy had had several Strats stolen and replaced at his own expense over the previous few months of touring, but as an established star by 1958 he no longer had to pay for them. Tommy Allsup, a few years older and a little wiser in the ways of the business, had a friend at the Fender company, who arranged for them to have two new Stratocasters and two new amplifiers, with Fender's compliments. Buddy's use of a Strat on the London Palladium show alone would have repaid Fender for all the guitars he could ever want, if he'd lived to be a hundred.

By now, Buddy was also carrying a small pistol. He was responsible for collecting the cash from promoters after their gigs, and with no intention of sending anything back to Norman Petty this meant he was carrying thousands of dollars around with him, much of it stuffed into the Lincoln's glove compartment. If J.I. or Joe B. needed cash, he'd just reach into the glove compartment and hand over a fistful of the stuff. The pistol was no big deal for a Texan (it wasn't even a very big pistol, only a .22), but if anybody tried to rob him, they'd be in for a surprise. The gun came into its own on at least one occasion after a show, when a car blocked the Lincoln as Buddy was trying to leave the car park. The car – whether containing would-be robbers or over-enthusiastic fans, we'll never know – roared off into the night when Buddy waved his pistol at them out of the Lincoln's window.

With cash in hand, there was no need for the Crickets to work in the summer of 1958, and J.I. and Buddy had marriage to contemplate. J.I. didn't waste much time contemplating; even though he and Buddy had talked of a double wedding, Jerry and

Peggy Sue decided they couldn't wait, and more or less eloped, marrying in Honey Grove, Texas, on 22 July. J. I.'s uncle Ray officiated. To make up for letting Buddy down over the double wedding, they suggested delaying their honeymoon until Buddy and Maria Elena had married, when the four of them could go to Acapulco together. Maria Elena arrived in Lubbock early in August, and was warmly welcomed by the Holley family in spite of the religious differences. 'We were all pleased with his pretty wife', says Larry Holley. The marriage took place on 15 August at the Holley house; afterwards, J.I. played Buddy's record of 'Now We're One' – appropriate lyrically, but possibly Holly's worst recording.

Hardly surprisingly, the joint honeymoon was pretty much a disaster. 'It was sort of uncomfortable', Allison remembers (*The Real Buddy Holly Story*). Peggy Sue, eighteen and just out of high school, never hit it off with the sophisticated New Yorker Maria Elena, seven years her senior, while J.I. annoyed both women as he tended to horse around as if they were on tour with the Crickets. The writing was clearly on the wall, and Buddy's other plans also showed how his life was changing. Before his marriage, Buddy had bought land in Lubbock and drawn up plans for a recording studio with a house attached to it to be built there; but the plan was for L.O. and Ella to live there, with L.O. looking after the studio, while Buddy made his home in New York with Maria Elena, visiting Lubbock to record, the way he had used the Clovis studio, and, more significantly, to produce other recording artists. He even intended to have his own pressing plant and delivery trucks – complete control of the records from the studio to the shops.

All these plans were eased by the fact that money from Peer–Southern flowed into the Crickets' account during August. A little over $28,000 flowed in, in five payments, and most of it flowed out again in Buddy's direction – J.I. got nearly $1,500 and Joc B. nearly $5,000. Buddy and Maria Elena set themselves up in a smart apartment a couple of blocks from Greenwich Village, paying a whopping rent of close to $1,000 per month. But while these changes in Buddy's life were going on, on 12 September the Crickets' single 'It's So Easy'/'Lonesome Tears' was released, and failed to chart at all either in the US or the UK, although it did reach number eight in Australia. Adding insult to injury, 'Ivan's' throwaway 'Real Wild Child', released on the same day, made number 68 on the Hot 100. The prospects of Buddy maintaining his new lifestyle very much depended on developing his career in new ways.

It's clear how Buddy saw his career developing. In the autumn of 1958 he set up his own publishing and record company, called Prism, and he intended to find and develop new talent, particularly from the West Texas area, recording at the studio in Lubbock. Ray Rush, from the Roses, joined Buddy in this venture. Until the studio was built, though, Buddy would continue to record in Clovis. The first person to benefit from this plan was a young DJ called Waylon Jennings, working at KLLL in Lubbock.

Earlier that year, the station had been bought by three brothers, Larry, Sky and Ray Corbin (known as 'Slim'). Hi Pockets Duncan had joined the staff, together with Jennings, who came from the town of Littlefield, 40 miles from Lubbock, and had aspirations to become a singer. They quickly made KLLL the top radio station in the area, concentrating on country music and western swing – rock 'n' roll was still regarded as a version of country music in those quarters. Naturally, Buddy would often drop in to the studio when he was in town, where he renewed acquaintance with old friends and made new ones; he already knew Waylon, who was just a year younger than Buddy and had often been along to the KDAV *Sunday Party* shows.

On 10 September 1958, Buddy, J.I. and Joe B. went along to Clovis to cut a couple of tracks with the saxophonist 'King' Curtis Ousley, who Buddy had met on the Alan Freed Paramount show. Curtis played the distinctive sax on many of the Coasters' records, such as 'Yakety Yak'. Buddy was already paying Curtis's expenses and fee for the session; now, he invited Waylon to come along to the session and to record two tracks of his own, again at Holly's expense.

The two Holly tracks were recorded first, with the usual Crickets line-up (Tommy Allsup wasn't present at the session, although Maria Elena was) plus King Curtis. They were 'Come Back Baby' (credited to Fred Neil and Norman Petty) and 'Reminiscing', written by King Curtis himself. Both are good, but 'Reminiscing' is simply superb, with Holly extending his vocal repertoire to include patterns used by the saxophone. They were the last songs he recorded in Clovis; neither was released in Holly's lifetime.

For Waylon Jennings' session, with Buddy as producer, Waylon sang while Buddy played guitar, with George Atwood on bass, Bo Clarke on drums, and King Curtis on tenor sax. They chose the Cajun standard 'Jole Blon' as the intended A-side of Waylon's first single. Although this is a great song, the choice was somewhat bizarre since it's sung in the Cajun

French dialect, and neither Buddy nor Waylon (nor anyone else on the session) knew the words. So Waylon based his version on a phonetic interpretation of what he heard on other recordings. The result is great fun – clearly everyone on the session had a good time – but essentially meaningless. The B-side, 'When Sin Stops', was an entirely presentable but unspectacular country number written by a local songwriter and guitarist, Bob Venable. The single was released by Brunswick, as a favour to Buddy, but made no impact.

Curiously, Buddy had earlier been refused permission to record 'When Sin Stops' himself. The band Bob Venable played guitar in, the Nighthawks, had recorded a demo of the song – complete with Holly-influenced 'hiccups' – at Norman Petty's studio. Buddy heard their version and wanted to record it himself, but needed the writer's permission because it had not yet been published. Even though Buddy was already a big star, he was turned down flat by Venable, who wanted to use the song to get a recording deal for his own band. They got their contract, and their record was released by Hamilton, a subsidiary of Dot Records, but wasn't a hit. Venable ended up as an oil man in Dallas. Once the song had been published, anyone could use it – but by that time, Buddy was more interested in finding material for Waylon than recording it himself.

Back in New York, Buddy worked with his second protégé, a young singer called Lou Giordano, who he had met through the Royal Teens. With Phil Everly as his co-producer, Buddy took Giordano into the Beltone studio in New York on 30 September 1958, to record the only Buddy Holly song that Holly never recorded even a demo of himself – 'Stay Close to Me'. The B-side was a Phil Everly composition, 'Don't Cha Know' (not the same as the song with this title later recorded by the post-Holly Crickets). Buddy and Phil both played guitar on the session, and joined Joey Villa, from the Royal Teens, on backing vocals; the other musicians on the session are not known. The records demonstrate that Lou Giordano was no Buddy Holly, and it's a pity that Buddy never recorded 'Stay Close to Me' himself; the best version was recorded much later by Mike Berry, in England. On the strength of the Holly connection, Giordano signed with Coral in November 1958 and the single was released on Brunswick in January 1959. It didn't achieve commercial success, and, in spite of several other attempts, nor did Lou. As things turned out, this was the end of Buddy Holly's career as a talent spotter and producer.

On 2 October, Buddy appeared on the Alan Freed *Dance Party* TV show, miming (lip-synching) 'It's So Easy'; the following day, he set off with J. I. and Joe B. on what proved to be their last tour together, as part of the grandiosely named *Biggest Show of Stars for 1958 – Fall Edition*. The other artists on the tour included Dion and the Belmonts, Jimmy Clanton, Frankie Avalon, Clyde McPhatter, Bobby Darin, Jack Scott, the Coasters, and Little Anthony and the Imperials.

But it wasn't like their earlier adventures. Tommy Allsup joined them as lead guitarist (but not, officially, a Cricket), the Roses came along to provide backing vocals, and Maria Elena was present, officially as Buddy's 'secretary' in order to preserve the illusion of his bachelorhood. She made her presence felt by taking charge of collecting the money from the gigs, proving to be a tough businesswoman (shades of Yoko Ono!) not easily conned by promoters trying to cheat her. Instead of the glove compartment of the car, the money now travelled in a plaid holdall dubbed the 'Scotch' bag; and instead of handfuls of cash being produced on demand, Maria Elena provided their entourage with regular payments, properly accounted for.

Although the tour was the usual crazy criss-crossing of several states, neither Buddy nor the other Crickets travelled on the tour bus. Buddy and Maria Elena had yet another new car, a taupe-coloured Cadillac, while J.I., Joe B. and Tommy, along with the three Roses, used the DeSoto station wagon (Buddy liked the grey-brown colour of his car so much that he decided to change the name of Prism to Taupe Records). This natural separation into two groups widened the distance between Buddy and his two younger buddies (Joe B. was still only eighteen, J.I. just nineteen), who were interested in getting drunk and messing around, while Buddy was becoming increasingly serious about his music and his career, and increasingly disillusioned with life on the road. By the end of the tour, he was talking of getting rid of Norman Petty and making his base in New York, preferably with J.I. and Joe B., provided they cleaned up their act. After the tour ended, on 19 October, Buddy's next recording session showed just how far he had come, musically speaking, in the past eighteen months.

For several months, Norman Petty had been trying to persuade Buddy to record with strings – something unheard of for a rock 'n' roller. Although initially unenthusiastic, Buddy was always interested in experimenting in the studio, and finally came round to accepting Petty's idea. The session was booked for

21 October 1958 at the Pythian Temple studio, with Dick Jacobs both producing and conducting the eighteen-piece orchestra – the songs would be recorded as live performances, with no overdubbing. For the session, Buddy and Norman had chosen Petty's song 'Moondreams', one written by the Everly Brothers' regular team Boudleaux and Felice Bryant, 'Raining In My Heart', and a Holly–Petty composition, 'True Love Ways'. There is considerable doubt over how much Petty contributed to the latter, which Buddy wrote for Maria Elena – the melody is based on one of his favourite gospel songs, 'I'll Be Alright' by the Angelic Gospel Singers, and the words are definitely all Buddy's.

Paul Anka had been promising to write a song specially for Buddy for some time, and a few hours before the session he came up with 'It Doesn't Matter Anymore'. Buddy loved it, and insisted it be included; because of the shortage of time, Dick Jacobs was able to arrange only a very simple pizzicato part for the violins.

There were plenty of people in the studio to watch, and hear, the 'new' Buddy Holly. Jerry Allison and Peggy Sue, Joe B., Norman and Vi Petty, Maria Elena and Paul Anka were all present. Peggy Sue remembers Buddy singing in an isolation booth to one side, visible through the glass window, while the orchestra played in the main studio; according to Dick Jacobs, though, he stood in front of the orchestra, just like a stage performance. Either way, the seasoned classical musicians in the orchestra initially took a superior attitude to what they regarded as a callow young pop singer, who couldn't even read music. But Buddy performed 'It Doesn't Matter Anymore' perfectly at the first time of asking – as far as Buddy's vocal contribution was concerned, most recordings really needed only one take – and their enthusiasm for the project and the singer visibly grew. 'I'd never heard Buddy sound so good', Peggy Sue recalls. 'It was like a mass of energy had engulfed me, and I could feel the music all the way down to my toes.' She stayed for the recording of 'Raining In My Heart', but Jerry, bored by the proceedings, dragged her away from the session before Buddy sang 'True Love Ways'. They missed a treat. Although the immediate reaction of most of the people present at the session was that 'Raining In My Heart' was the best song, posterity has rightly given the accolade to 'True Love Ways', which has become a standard, recorded by many artists in many ways, but none as good as the original. It doesn't even need strings – Buddy's country roots show clearly in the version recorded many years later by the Mavericks.

Apart from the quality of the songs and the performance, there was something else special about the session. Unknown to anyone in the studio where the recordings were made, Coral sound engineers were taking a feed to another studio, where they made experimental stereo recordings of the songs. Those tapes, labelled 'Do Not Use', gathered dust on the shelves for years before they were discovered, resulting eventually in the release of the only Buddy Holly recordings made in true stereo. They were also, as it turned out, his last official studio recordings.

One week after the Pythian Temple session, all three of the Crickets appeared on *American Bandstand*, lip-synching their latest releases: Buddy's 'Heartbeat' (released on 5 November with 'Well … All Right' as the B-side, it reached only number 82 in the Hot 100 and number 30 in the UK), and the Crickets' 'It's So Easy' (released on 12 September). It was the last time they performed together.

Before returning to Lubbock, Buddy talked over his plans with J. I. and Joe B. The three of them would break with Norman Petty, demand that he hand over the money in the Crickets' bank account, and use this to establish themselves in New York, as well as building a recording studio in Lubbock. The younger Crickets agreed that they would all act together and confront Petty as a group. Unfortunately, they flew back to Texas immediately, while Buddy and Maria Elena drove down in the Cadillac. With nothing much to do in Lubbock, J.I. and Joe B. went over to Clovis to hang out at the studio, and let the cat out of the bag. Before Buddy arrived back on the scene, Petty had persuaded the teenagers that they would be better off living in Texas, that the sharks in New York would rip them off and steal their royalties (something Norman knew all about), and that if Buddy wanted a solo career, well, they could carry on as the Crickets – after all, Buddy's name wasn't even on the contract the Crickets had signed when they did a deal on the back of 'That'll Be The Day'. And who had got them that deal? Good old Norman, of course.

Joe B. has offered the clearest account of what happened at their meeting with Petty (*Memories*):

Norman said, 'Look, let's stay down here where we have control of everything.' And he had us built up, saying, 'You guys are the Crickets, you will be the Crickets and you'll keep the Crickets name. And we'll get another lead singer and a guitar player' – so forth and so on. He told us that the Crickets were the ones that had had all the hits – Buddy Holly only had 'Peggy Sue', and he couldn't make a living on the name Buddy Holly. So if we stayed down in Clovis with Norman, we could keep the name the Crickets, and Norman had – quote – 'all his money in the bank and we'll starve him to death' – unquote.

Allison puts it more succinctly: 'We wanted to be a group [with Buddy], but Norman Petty, the fact is, talked us out of it. That's the straight deal.' (*The Real Buddy Holly Story*)

Peggy Sue tells how Jerry broke the news to Buddy, over a Coke at the Busy Bee Cafe in Clovis, saying that he couldn't stand the idea of living in New York, of being unable to ride his motorcycle or have the freedom he had in Texas. Buddy asked about Joe B. 'I'll take care of him. We'll be the Crickets, and you go be Buddy Holly', she recalls him saying. And Buddy replied, 'All right, man. If that's what you're going to do. If that's the way you want it', and walked out. 'I sat there beside Jerry, dumbfounded. I had worried about Maria trying to fire him, and here *he* had fired *Buddy*. If he didn't want to live in New York that was one thing, but to fire Buddy! I never expected this.'

On 5 November, just before returning to New

York, Buddy had his first (and only) flying lesson, following enthusiastically in the trail of Larry Holley, who had recently qualified as a pilot.

With the break-up of the band, Petty now had another excuse not to release any money from the Crickets' account to Buddy – he said that it couldn't be distributed until the situation was resolved. Buddy figured that the only way to resolve it was by legal action. Back in New York, he found that the Everly Brothers were having similar problems with their own manager, Wesley Rose (the man who wouldn't let them record 'Wishing' and 'Love's Made A Fool Of You'), and hired their lawyer, Harold Orenstein, who was a specialist in such show-business 'divorces'. In the long run, Petty would undoubtedly have to hand over the money he legally owed Buddy, even if he managed to hang on to some which was legally his but morally Buddy's. Just how much was at stake can be gleaned from an estimate made by Larry Lehmer of the contribution from 'That'll Be The Day' alone. Based on sales of 1 million, with both sides of the record counting for royalties to both the performers and the credited songwriters, plus other rights, Lehmer calculated that Petty was entitled to $32,333, Buddy to $17,333, J. I. to $12,333 and Joe B. and Niki Sullivan (who didn't even play on the record!) to $9,000 each. Petty was actually making almost twice as much from the record as Buddy, thanks to his songwriting credits, 50 per cent publishing share, and agent's percentage. He was also, we now know, taking 40 per cent of the Crickets' money and not tithing it. Add that to the pot, and he was taking more than the band!

Whatever the long-term ramifications, in the short term Buddy and Maria Elena had to survive, and they were broke but living in an expensive apartment in New York. They were kept afloat by the generosity of Aunt Provi, who certainly must have known, through her inside contacts, roughly how much was owed to Buddy. It came as a shock to all concerned in New York when correspondence between Orenstein and Petty revealed that there wasn't, in fact, a 'Crickets' bank account, but an account in the name of the Norman Petty Agency into which the money had flowed, with such a shambolic paper trail (perhaps deliberately so) that even if there had been goodwill on both sides, there could have been no swift resolution of the situation.

But life went on. Buddy loved living in New York, hanging out in cafés in bohemian Greenwich Village in the small hours of the night, watching and meeting other musicians, learning and planning future projects. His bubbling creativity carried over into his songwriting, and recording demos and rehearsal tapes in the apartment on Fifth Avenue. Although the results are sometimes referred to as 'home recordings', the tape machine Buddy had at home was actually the same Ampex machine that Norman Petty had used in Clovis and in sessions on the road, including the one at Tinker Air Force Base that produced the hit version of 'Maybe Baby'. Petty was in the process of upgrading his studio (where did he get the money, I wonder?) and had sold (that's right, *sold*) the Ampex machine to Buddy.

Accompanying himself on acoustic guitar, on 3 December 1958 Buddy recorded 'That's What They Say' and 'What To Do'. Two days later, he recorded 'Peggy Sue Got Married' and 'That Makes It Tough'. In a letter to his parents dated 11 December, Buddy mentioned that he had been writing some 'fairly good' songs. 'The best one to date is a "top secret" one titled "Peggy Sue Got Married". Please don't mention it to anyone either. I want it to be a complete surprise.' On 14 December, it was the turn of 'Crying, Waiting, Hoping', and on 17 December 'Learning the Game', the last of the six new Holly songs on the 'Apartment Tapes', as they became known, was recorded.

During the fortnight he was writing and recording these songs, Buddy was also making arrangements to do something about his temporary
shortage of cash. The only solution to the problem
was to go on the road. He got in touch with GAC,
who quickly fixed him up as the headline act on a
Winter Dance Party tour of the Midwest. He would be
the main attraction, supported by Ritchie Valens,
who had a double-sided hit single with 'Donna' / 'La
Bamba', a DJ and songwriter called J.P. Richardson,
but known as the Big Bopper, whose big record was
'Chantilly Lace', old friends Dion and the Belmonts,
and a young singer named Frankie Sardo who had a
pleasant voice but never made the big time. The
three-week tour would begin on 23 January, which
gave Buddy time to enjoy Christmas and the New
Year with his family and Maria Elena, but barely
time to recruit – let alone rehearse – the musicians to
accompany him in place of J.I. and Joe B.

Putting his problems to one side, with the help of
Aunt Provi and an advance from GAC against his
tour income, Buddy put on a show of being a successful rock star when he arrived in Lubbock with
Maria Elena for Christmas 1958. He brought lavish
presents, and home movies from Christmas Day
itself show him joining in the family fun seemingly

without a care in the world. Larry Holley remembers that Christmas as 'a wonderful time', and cherishes the memory of Buddy singing 'Raining In My Heart' for him, accompanied only by his acoustic guitar: 'I liked it best just like he did it in Lubbock.' Buddy also saw old friends, including Jack Neal, and even visited Clovis to see Bob Montgomery, who was working as a sound engineer in Petty's studio. But he made no attempt to contact J.I. and Joe B., who were now living in Clovis themselves.

He also had to find their replacements. Obviously Tommy Allsup would play lead guitar on the tour, and Tommy recommended a young drummer called Carl Bunch to join them. Bunch, who had just turned eighteen, had been recording in Clovis, where Tommy had been doing session work, with a band called Ronnie Smith and the Poor Boys. 'That's like being offered to take Ringo's place in the Beatles', he says (*The Definitive Story*). What would you do? Carl quit high school to take the job. That left Buddy with the problem of finding a bass player. His solution was to tell Waylon Jennings that he'd got the job, even though Waylon had never played bass in his life. Swept along by Buddy's enthusiasm, in three weeks Waylon would learn not how to play bass, but where to put his fingers to play the required notes for all Buddy's hits. It was only halfway through the tour, he later recalled, that he realised that the electric bass is essentially just like the top four strings on an ordinary electric guitar (that is, the four deepest notes) and he could start learning to play the thing properly. Not that he ever did learn how to play it properly – almost all the pictures of the group on stage during that last tour show Tommy Allsup looking towards Waylon, checking up on him and giving him a signal when it was time to make the changes.

Buddy's songwriting ability overflowed on 27 December, when he was hanging out at KLLL with Waylon and Slim Corbin. After he'd been bragging in a good-natured fashion about how easy it was to write a song, he was challenged to prove it, and came up with 'You're The One' in the space of fifteen minutes. With Buddy singing and playing acoustic guitar and the other two providing handclaps (or possibly slapping their thighs, not always exactly in time), the three of them cut an acetate of the song there and then, which Buddy generously credited as a Holly–Jennings–Corbin composition. It's the last song he ever wrote; certainly a simple one, but an entirely acceptable addition to the Buddy Holly songbook. He really could write songs to order, which was one reason why he was so generous with the writing credits – he could always write another one, so what did it matter? But as Larry Holley says, perhaps understandably taking a rather extreme view, everyone knows who wrote the Crickets' songs. 'Did they [J. I., Joe B. and Norman Petty] ever come up with any good songs after Buddy died? Anyone with any discernment knows who wrote the songs.'

After the holiday festivities, it was time to get back to New York, put his business affairs in order as best he could, and prepare for the winter tour. On 5 January, Coral released 'It Doesn't Matter Anymore' backed with 'Raining In My Heart' (for some incomprehensible reason, one of Buddy's best recordings relegated to a B-side); but it failed to make any immediate impact on the charts. The original plan had been for Maria Elena to accompany Buddy on the tour, just as she had in October; but when she told Buddy that she had just discovered she was pregnant, the delighted father-to-be insisted that she should stay at home and rest while he was on the road. Resting was the last thing on his own mind, though. As if he wasn't busy enough already, during the first three weeks of January 1959 (the exact dates are not known) Buddy recorded several non-original songs on the Ampex machine. Half a dozen or so survive; there is tantalising evidence from snippets on the tape that he also recorded other songs, but re-used the tape after playing them back.

The surviving songs are the standard 'Wait 'Til The Sun Shines Nellie' (which was the template for 'That's What They Say', as anyone with any discernment can tell), both slow and fast versions of Little Richard's 'Slippin' and Slidin'', 'Dearest' (also known as 'Umm, Oh Yeah'), Mickey and Sylvia's 'Love is Strange', a Leiber–Stoller song, 'Smokey Joe's Cafe', a fragment of 'Drown in My Own Tears', and an instrumental, Ray Charles' 'Leave My Woman Alone'. From the order of the material on the tapes, this instrumental, sometimes known as 'Buddy's Guitar', was probably the last recording Buddy Holly ever made. Tommy Allsup, Waylon Jennings and Carl Bunch were in New York to rehearse with Buddy at a studio he rented for a week before the tour; it's possible that Waylon or Tommy are playing guitar on some of these recordings. When he wasn't rehearsing with the others, Bunch spent every minute he could playing along with Holly's records, trying to duplicate J. I.'s sound.

The slow and fast versions of 'Slippin' and Slidin'' are particularly interesting, and thereby hangs a tale.

Novelty records often do well at Christmas time, and the big Christmas hit of 1958 in the US was 'The Chipmunk Song', which featured the multi-tracked, speeded-up voice of singer-songwriter David Seville. Buddy was always fascinated by recording technology (witness his wire recordings at the age of twelve, and the experimental techniques used on 'Words of Love'), and it's now clear that he intended the slow version of 'Slippin' and Slidin'' to be speeded up to produce a Chipmunks effect. This explains why he recorded it at a tape speed of 7½ inches per second (IPS) instead of the usual 15 IPS. But nobody realised this until a producer at MCA, Steve Hoffman, was working with the Holly material in 1984, and made the connection!

In fact, simply playing the recording at double speed doesn't produce an entirely satisfactory sound, because it alters the pitch. But a musician friend of mine, Warwick Bilton, used some modern electronic trickery to produce several different speeded-up versions of the song, and we discovered that sped up and pitched up by 5 per cent it produces a really good sound. This is my favourite and probably what Buddy had in mind, as it's a major sixth up so musically sounds 'right', with the tempo very close to that of the 'fast' version. All of which meant that we could hear a 'new' Buddy Holly recording almost 50 years after his death; more significantly, it gives us some insight into his love of innovation and his playful state of mind early in 1959.

His mood changed, though, as the time for the *Winter Dance Party* tour approached. On legal advice, he was being billed on the tour as 'Buddy Holly and the Crickets', to maintain his claim to the Crickets' name and the income associated with it, as a lever in his legal battle with Norman Petty; but even this was a reminder that the only reason he was going on the tour was because Petty had got his affairs tied up in legal hassles. The night before Buddy left to join the tour, he and Maria Elena both had bad dreams. Hers involved a fireball coming out of the sky and crashing in front of her; his involved flying in a small plane with Larry Holley and Maria Elena, but being persuaded by Larry to land and leave her behind before flying off again.

Their actual parting, a few hours later as Buddy set off to join 'the Crickets' for the tour, was a sombre affair. Maria Elena tried to persuade Buddy to take her along, even packing her suitcase and lying that she felt fine and wasn't suffering from morning sickness, but he insisted that she stayed, for the sake of the baby. 'One thing I always have in mind,' she told

Philip Norman, 'and that I'll always regret, is that I wasn't more determined, that I didn't insist more. Because I know that if I would have gone with him, Buddy would never have taken that plane.'

The musicians travelled by train to Chicago to meet up with the other artists and run through some quick rehearsals, then on by bus to Milwaukee for the first gig on 23 January 1959. Holly's new band were the only really professional, competent musicians, and had to provide backing for most of the other acts, as well as doing their own set. The itinerary involved the usual insane cat's-cradle crisscrossing of the country, literally doubling back on itself several times. It would have been ridiculous in summer, in comfortable air-conditioned buses. On some occasions, they had to travel 400 miles through the night immediately after a gig and into the next day, arriving at the venue with barely time to unpack and set up for the next show. What made things worse was that it was the height of a particularly severe winter, said to have been the worst in the Midwest for 30 years – it was so cold, said Waylon Jennings (VH1), that 'what you do is you hold your breath from the time you left the bus until you got to the dressing room door' – and that the tour organisers had hired the cheapest available bus, which turned out to be a retired school bus, too decrepit to be used for ferrying children any more. The roads were just two-lane country roads; no modern super-highways. When the first bus inevitably broke down, it was replaced by a similar vehicle – and so on, eight times with eight different buses in ten days, according to Tommy Allsup, often with no working heater (Carl Bunch remembers twelve broken-down buses, but maybe it just felt like twelve).

The one bright spot was that there was no booking for 2 February; after ten days on the road, the performers would at least get a day off and a chance to do their laundry. Or so they thought, until they heard that GAC, eager to make every penny they could, had managed to fill this hole in the schedule with a booking at the Surf Ballroom in Clear Lake, Iowa – a mere 350 miles from the gig in Green Bay, Wisconsin, on 1 February. The next day, 3 February, they were expected to be in Moorhead, Minnesota, well over 400 miles from Clear Lake.

With all this going on, the music was a great success. Buddy in particular, though missing Maria Elena, was happy to be cutting free from Norman Petty, making plans for a European tour, and making friends with Ritchie Valens, who he planned to sign to Prism/Taupe Records. At least twice a day, Buddy phoned Maria Elena; at every show, if there was a telephone near the stage he would get Ritchie to hold it up for her to listen while he sang 'True Love Ways'.

Carl Bunch remembers the basic set that they played each night. They always opened with 'Gotta Travel On', which Buddy played on his own, and followed with 'That'll Be The Day', 'Everyday', 'Maybe Baby', 'It Doesn't Matter Anymore', 'True Love Ways', 'Peggy Sue', 'Oh Boy!', 'Brown Eyed Handsome Man', 'It's So Easy', 'Not Fade Away', 'Bo Diddley', and 'Rave On' (another great iPod playlist). Sometimes they included Little Richard numbers, or something by Jerry Lee Lewis, or Gene Vincent's 'Be-Bop-A-Lula', which must have brought back memories of Nashville. But the set list wasn't actually 'set' – Buddy was confident enough to read the mood of an audience and choose which number to play next accordingly. He never got it wrong, and nobody sat down while Buddy Holly was on stage. The crowds of enthusiastic youngsters who were given such a treat included, on 31 January in Duluth, Minnesota, seventeen-year-old Robert Zimmerman, who would soon change his name to Bob Dylan, and who would one day record 'Gotta Travel On' himself.

By the time the tour reached Clear Lake on 2 February, although they were still capable of putting on a show to bring the house down, the performers were physically in a sorry state. The Bopper had a heavy, flu-like cold and Carl Bunch had been hospitalised with frost-bitten feet the day before, after the latest bus broke down in the early hours of 1 February and they were stranded in temperatures of 30 below freezing (Fahrenheit) with no heating (the wind chill made it equivalent to minus 40). The rest were in marginally better shape, but they were all exhausted and their clothes were so filthy that Waylon Jennings later said, using only mild hyperbole, that his shirts could stand up by themselves. Buddy had had enough, and on the way to Clear Lake he hatched a plan to hire a light aircraft to take himself and the two remaining 'Crickets' on to Moorhead after the show, giving them a chance to get cleaned up, eat a proper hot meal, and sleep. The plan was crystallised when it turned out that the manager of the Surf Ballroom, Carroll Anderson, was a friend of Jerry Dwyer, who ran a flying service at nearby Mason City airport, and could book the flight for him to Fargo, the nearest airport to Moorhead.

For the show itself, performed to an ecstatic audience of about 1,300 people at the Surf Ballroom, the absence of Carl Bunch meant that drumming duties had to be shared by anyone who knew which end of a stick to hold and wasn't required up front, and Buddy enthusiastically took his turn. Dion and the Belmonts performed just before Buddy closed the show, with Buddy carefully hidden in the shadows playing drums. After the set, with the kids already screaming for Buddy, Dion went through the routine of introducing all the band members, 'forgetting' the drummer. When prompted, he said: 'Oh, that's our new drummer – Buddy Holly.' Stepping out of the shadows to a roar of applause, Buddy picked up his guitar and sang 'Gotta Travel On'. Waylon then joined him for 'Salty Dog Blues', an old bluegrass favourite, before Buddy, with his full backing band including Ritchie Valens on drums, launched into the Holly/Crickets hits. As a finale, he was joined by Ritchie and the Bopper, sweating profusely from his flu but gamely keeping up with the others, in a ragged but raucous version of 'La Bamba'. It was the last song Buddy Holly ever performed.

Even before the show, the ailing Bopper had persuaded Waylon Jennings to give up his seat on the plane to him, because he was too sick to stand another night on the bus. Throughout the evening, Ritchie Valens, who was still only seventeen, and who idolised Buddy and had never flown on a small plane, had been pestering Tommy Allsup to let him take the last seat in the plane. At the last minute, Tommy agreed to toss a coin for the seat – he flipped it, and Ritchie called 'heads'. The 50 cent piece came up heads. 'That's the first time in my life I ever won anything', said Ritchie.

As Buddy and his friends were getting ready to leave for the airport, Waylon came up to say good-bye to Buddy. Much later, he described their last words together.

'Well,' laughed Buddy, 'I hear you're not coming on the plane with us.'

'No', said Waylon.

'Well, I hope your ol' bus freezes up!'

'Yeah, and I hope your ol' plane crashes.'

This piece of light-hearted banter would haunt Waylon Jennings for the rest of his life.

The three performers were in high spirits when they arrived at Mason City airport, looking forward to the prospect of a comfortable hotel room and a hot bath. The real tragedy of the situation is that it doesn't seem to have occurred to anyone that they could have got these comforts locally, resting, eating and getting cleaned up first, before taking a plane to Moorhead in daylight hours, during the afternoon of

3 February. But as any performer will tell you, it's hard to come down after a successful gig, and the adrenalin surge of performing probably coloured their desire to travel on as quickly as possible.

There's no mystery about why the plane crashed. The official report of the Civil Aeronautics Board (CAB) provides a clear and compelling reconstruction of what went wrong. As is usually the case with aircraft accidents, several factors conspired to cause the tragedy. The aircraft itself was a four-seat Beechcraft Bonanza, with a 'V' tail configuration. Although a fine aircraft, the type was known for its sensitivity, requiring a light touch on the controls; according to the 1981 edition of *The Aviation Consumer Used Aircraft Guide*, 'once a wing dips a little, it tends to keep going. In instrument weather and turbulence, this low rolling stability can put the pilot into the "graveyard spiral" very quickly.' On this particular occasion, the aircraft was probably loaded incorrectly. With two passengers in the back, the centre of gravity of the Bonanza would have been very close to the recommended rear limit, and as well as the passengers and their luggage, it was crammed with dirty laundry that Buddy, the Bopper and Ritchie had promised to get cleaned for their fellow performers. There was a total of 42 pounds of baggage, filling the luggage compartment and overflowing into the back of the cockpit with Ritchie and the Bopper. Buddy, of course, sat up front, next to the pilot. Moving the centre of gravity back in this way wouldn't have stopped the plane flying, but as the *Guide* puts it, 'an aft c.g. further reduces the V-tail's already low longitudinal stability, making the airplane even more sensitive,' and 'an out of c.g. Bonanza can really take a pilot by surprise'.

A skilled pilot could have coped with all that. The next problem was that Roger Peterson, the pilot chosen by Jerry Dwyer, although competent and experienced at flying in normal visibility, was not skilled when it came to night-flying on instruments. Only 21, and having held a commercial pilot's licence for less than a year (although he had been flying for four), he was not, in fact, qualified to fly on instruments. Although he had had more than 50 hours of training in instrument flying, wearing dark goggles to simulate low visibility, he had never satisfied his instructors that he was safe. His instructors described him as 'below average', and one said that when he became distracted he began 'allowing the aircraft to go into diving spirals to the right'. These problems may have been exacerbated by hearing deficiencies. Routine medicals showed that he had a loss of hearing in lower ranges in his left ear in October 1956, and in March 1958 problems were noticed with his right ear. He was allowed to continue flying in spite of these problems after passing a flight test in November 1958. But his Airman's Certificate, dated 8 November 1958, specifically stated that 'holder does not meet night-flight requirements' for instrument flying.

Even for a pilot skilled in flying on instruments, those in the Bonanza could cause confusion. The instrument that showed whether the plane was climbing or descending, a Sperry Attitude Gyro, worked the other way round from the one Peterson had encountered when he was training. It's possible – even likely – that once he was out of sight of the ground he misread the instrument and thought his plane was climbing when in fact it was descending.

Then there was the weather. At 23:35 on 2 February and 00:15 on 3 February, the US Weather Bureau issued 'flash' weather warnings of a band of snow moving into the area, with strong, gusty winds, poor visibility, and icing. Neither of these reports was passed on to Peterson by his local air traffic control, although there was freezing fog around and light snow was already falling by the time the plane was loaded and sitting at the end of the runway with clearance to take off.

It sat there for several minutes, roughly between 00:50 and 00:55 on 3 February 1959. Dwyer, who had come along to check that everything went smoothly, was puzzled by the delay, which has never been explained; it's possible that Peterson was having second thoughts about proceeding with the flight, and was being persuaded by Buddy and the others, who had already literally missed the bus to their next gig, that they should carry on. Whoever made it, 'the decision to go,' says the CAB report, 'seems most imprudent.'

But the decision was made, and Jerry Dwyer – who, surely, should either have cancelled the flight or, as a much more experienced pilot, taken the job himself – watched from the control tower as his aircraft made a normal take-off and continued rising into the dark ebony sky. 'When the airplane was directly North of the field, I noticed by watching the white tail light in reference to the red lights on the two towers on the North edge of the field the airplane appeared to be going down at a very slow rate of descent as it went farther away from us. I would guess that it was approximately four miles North of us. I thought at the time that probably it was an optical illusion.'

It wasn't. The aircraft was going down at its cruising speed of about 170 miles an hour. It crashed into a field five miles north-west of Mason City airport at about 01:00 local time, on 3 February 1959. All on board were killed instantly.

CHAPTER SIX

Not Fade Away

When Buddy Holly died, he was 22 years and five months old. It's impossible to say what he would have achieved if he'd lived, but there's one apposite example which shows what might have been. When John Lennon was 22 years and five months old, in March 1963, the Beatles had just had their first number one on the *New Musical Express* chart with a John Lennon song, 'Please Please Me', and their first album, named after the single, had just been released. It was four years after Buddy Holly died, but Lennon wasn't yet in the same league as Holly; his career was at the same stage Buddy's had been in the summer of 1957. The way Lennon's career and that of his partner Paul McCartney developed over the next four years, up to and including the release of the album *Sergeant Pepper's Lonely Hearts Club Band*, gives just a hint of what a talent like Holly's might have produced.

What actually happened in the aftermath of 3 February 1959 was that 'It Doesn't Matter Anymore' rose to number thirteen in the Hot 100 and number one in the UK (where it sold just over 400,000 copies) for six weeks, while 'Raining In My Heart' charted in its own right in the US, reaching number 88. They were Buddy's last American hit singles – but he soon had his first American hit album, when Coral hastily put together a 'best of' LP called *The Buddy Holly Story*. This was an excellent compilation containing 'Raining In My Heart', 'Early In The Morning', 'Peggy Sue', 'Maybe Baby', 'Everyday', 'Rave On', 'Heartbeat', 'Think It Over', 'Oh Boy!', 'It's So Easy', and 'It Doesn't Matter Anymore'. The only quibble might be that the songs are not presented in chronological order, but few of the fans who kept the album in the charts for years, on and off, would have been bothered by that. It reached number eleven in the US, and number two in the UK – the *South Pacific* soundtrack album was number one in the UK throughout the whole of 1959. But *The Buddy Holly Story* spent 156 weeks on the UK chart itself.

Meanwhile, after Buddy's death Norman Petty had no difficulty in establishing the right of Joe B. Mauldin and Jerry Allison to the name 'the Crickets' (in the end, Jerry Allison ended up with sole rights to the name, which he still holds), but considerably more difficulty getting them the success he had promised. With Sonny Curtis on guitar and a young vocalist called Earl Sinks, they had recorded just two tracks in Clovis – their version of 'Love's Made A Fool Of You', and 'Someone, Someone' – which had been delivered to New York but not released, partly because of the legal hassles.

By February 1959, J.I. and Joe B. were disillusioned with Petty and trying to get back with Buddy, who had told them 'it only takes a phone call'. Jerry tried to make that call on 2 February, speaking to Maria Elena in New York, then trying but failing to get in touch with Buddy in Clear Lake. Buddy never got the message. Although 'Love's Made A Fool Of You' was issued under the Crickets' name once Buddy was not around to object, it did nothing in the US and reached only number 26 in the UK. The group split from Norman Petty and headed out to make their base in Los Angeles. Joe B. took with him $10,000 as a settlement from Petty. 'I was sure it ought to have been more,' he told Philip Norman, 'but my accountant told me, "Norman's books are in such a mess, you'd better take what you can."' The Holly estate had received $70,000 shortly after his death – more than enough, if he'd had it when he split with Petty, to have saved his life. The surviving Crickets also tried to sort out the confusion surrounding the songwriting credits; most notably, J.I. got his share of 'Peggy Sue' reduced to 10 per cent, with Buddy's share correspondingly increased; it has cost him a small fortune, but he has never regretted it.

Over the years, the post-Holly Crickets suffered many personnel changes, which didn't help them to establish a name in their own right, and they were particularly hard hit when Sonny Curtis, like Elvis before him, had to do his compulsory military service. Through everything, they retained a strong fan following in the UK, although for long periods they were essentially forgotten in their homeland. Along the way, Curtis and Allison wrote 'More Than I Can Say', the best Buddy Holly song not actually written by Buddy, and the Crickets backed the Everly Brothers (for whom Curtis wrote 'Walk Right Back') both on tour and on record (J.I.'s distinctive drumming is particularly prominent on their records 'Till I Kissed You' and 'Cathy's Clown').

In spite of successful solo careers, the core of Allison, Curtis and Mauldin continued to perform as the Crickets from time to time, and to cut records up to the end of the century and beyond; their last release (so far) is a superb album, *The Crickets and Their Buddies*, featuring guest contributions on fifteen songs associated with Buddy Holly and the Crickets.

Waylon Jennings also had a successful musical career – eventually, the most successful of any of Buddy's entourage. After some well-documented hard times in the 1960s, he became a major country star, and formed the Highwaymen with Willie Nelson, Johnny Cash and Kris Kristofferson. But he never forgot his last words to Buddy, and late in life he said, 'if anything I've ever done is remembered, part of it is because of Buddy Holly … he was the first guy who had confidence in me.' In his autobiography, Waylon recalls Buddy telling him about the disastrous Nashville sessions, and saying: 'Don't ever let people tell you you can't do something, and never put limits on yourself.' When Waylon was recording in Nashville himself many years later, sometimes the engineers would sneer: '"Man, that sounds like a pop hit." And I'd remember Buddy talking to me, telling me they thought he was crazy, as that freezing bus moved down the highway from Green Bay, Wisc., to Clear Lake, Iowa.' In the 1970s, when the Crickets were based near Nashville, Jennings used them as musicians in the studio, and took them along as a support act on his tours. He died, from complications caused by diabetes, on 13 February 2002.

Tommy Allsup continued his career as a session musician, moving into record production. He still tours, with Kevin Montgomery, Bob Montgomery's son. Bob Montgomery himself had a hugely success-ful career both as a songwriter (his many hits include Patsy Cline's 'Back in Baby's Arms' and Cliff Richard's 'Wind Me Up') and as a publisher and pro-ducer. Among his biggest successes, his company published 'The Wind Beneath My Wings', and he pro-duced Bobby Goldsboro's 'Honey'. Bob's career, in fact, very closely followed the path that Buddy had mapped out for himself by the beginning of 1959, although, with no disrespect to Bob, we might guess that Buddy would have been even more influential.

The last member of the *Winter Dance Party* 'Crickets', Carl Bunch, failed to make a long-term career in music, even though at one time he played drums for Roy Orbison and later with Hank Williams Jr. In the 1970s he experienced a moment of epi-phany and subsequently became a minister, work-ing as a substance abuse counsellor.

Back in 1959, the success of *The Buddy Holly Story* prompted Coral to try to make something that they regarded as commercial out of the six demos Holly had recorded in the New York apartment, and which Maria Elena had passed over to them. In June 1959, Dick Jacobs gave the job to his assistant, Jack Hansen, who tried to emulate what he thought of as the Crickets' sound by overdubbing not just guitar, bass and drums, but 'backing' vocals in the style of the Picks and the Roses. The results were OK, but clearly nothing like the way Buddy Holly would have completed the recordings. At the time, Buddy Holly fans (especially in the UK) were just pleased that there was some new material to listen to. After 'It Doesn't Matter Anymore' slipped down the chart and before the new material was released, one of the old Nashville recordings, 'Midnight Shift', was released as a single in the UK, reaching number 26 and emphasising the thirst for Holly records in that part of the world – and in Australia, where it made number seven!

The overdubbed recordings were the core of a second Holly compilation, *The Buddy Holly Story Volume Two*, which contained 'Peggy Sue Got Married', 'Well ... All Right', 'What To Do', 'That Makes It Tough', 'Now We're One', 'Take Your Time', 'Crying, Waiting, Hoping', 'True Love Ways', 'Little Baby', 'Moondreams', and 'That's What They Say'. It seems to have been put together rather carelessly; 'Fool's

Paradise' and 'Lonesome Tears' would have made much stronger contributions than 'Now We're One' and 'Little Baby'. The album did well, especially in Britain where it reached number seven, but not on the same scale as *The Buddy Holly Story*. The single 'Peggy Sue Got Married'/'Crying, Waiting, Hoping' didn't chart at all in the US but reached number thirteen in the UK, while an album of the Nashville sessions under the title *That'll Be The Day* went to number five on the British LP chart.

For the next three years, although Buddy Holly's name disappeared entirely from the charts in the United States, every year he had hit records in Britain. In 1960, a re-issue of 'Heartbeat' got to number 30, 'True Love Ways' reached number 25, and 'Learning the Game' made it to 36. In 1961, 'What To Do' got to 34, followed by a double-sided hit with 'You're So Square'/'Valley of Tears' that soared all the way to number twelve. But in 1962 something sensational happened, as far as Holly fans were concerned. In March, a re-issue of 'Listen to Me' just tiptoed in to the charts for one week at number 48, and it looked as if the well had finally run dry; but in September a 'brand-new' studio recording by Buddy Holly was released. It was 'Reminiscing', and it rose to number seventeen, signalling a Buddy Holly resurgence in

1963, the year of the Beatles' big breakthrough.

Buddy also had a hit by proxy in September 1962. I vividly recall feeling personally affronted when 'Sheila', Tommy Roe's blatant rip-off of 'Peggy Sue', got to number three, although now it seems more like a tribute to Buddy Holly. But the swift response of the Crickets, whose 'My Little Girl' managed to recreate the feel of 'Peggy Sue' and also include musical allusions to 'Sheila', made me feel much better when it hit the charts in January 1963.

It had taken so long for 'Reminiscing' to be released, in spite of its obvious commercial potential, because of the legal tangle that Holly's musical legacy had been left in. There were the Apartment Tapes in New York, various recordings left at his parents' home and other locations in Lubbock, and high-quality material, including 'Reminiscing', in Norman Petty's possession. Some difficulties were easily and amicably resolved. Because Buddy had died without leaving a will, his entire estate went to his wife, Maria Elena. But once she had recovered from the immediate shock of his death (which made her lose the baby she was carrying), she promptly made over half of it to his family in Lubbock. Other matters, including the question of how much money Petty owed Buddy, were less easily, and less amicably, resolved. But it was only after they were resolved that decisions could be made about the musical legacy.

Petty, of course, continued to work with other artists, and in 1961 one of them, a group he dubbed the String-A-Longs, had a big hit with 'Wheels', an instrumental he'd written. The number had been rejected by his regular house band of the time, the Fireballs – but he soon found something else for them to do.

When the time did come to do something with the music left behind by Buddy Holly, sorting out who owned what rights to the recordings, and what to do with them, produced an uneasy marriage of convenience. Eventually, it was agreed that everything would be turned over to Norman Petty to be tidied up and, where possible, made suitable for release. There wasn't really any choice, regardless of what Maria Elena, in particular, felt about Norman. Petty had physical possession of much of the material, he was a good producer who, unlike Jack Hansen, had known Buddy's style of working, and the Holleys were frightened of being ripped off by the suits in New York. The deal would see income from the future Buddy Holly releases split three ways, between the Holleys, Petty, and Maria Elena, with Petty regaining artistic control of Buddy Holly's recordings.

The first fruit of the deal was the release of the 'Reminiscing' single, followed a few months later by an album of the same name, which reached number two in the UK chart (held off the top only by the Beatles) and number 40 in the US. The album spawned the hit versions of 'Brown Eyed Handsome Man' (UK number three) and 'Bo Diddley' (UK number four) which nestled in the charts in the spring and summer of 1963, four years after his death, alongside such artists as the Beatles, Gerry and the Pacemakers, and the Searchers – all of whom had been inspired by Buddy. 'Brown Eyed Handsome Man' actually sold more copies in the UK (159,000) than Buddy's 1958 classic 'Rave On' (150,000).

But although Norman Petty's work on the tapes was an improvement on that of Jack Hansen, it was far from perfect. Both 'Brown Eyed Handsome Man', from the Clovis session which first made Petty sit up and take notice of Buddy, and other tracks were needlessly overdubbed, although admittedly some of the additions to 'Bo Diddley', in particular the maracas, do help. The track selection was also rather odd, with some of the last songs recorded in New York ('Wait Till The Sun Shines Nellie' and 'Slippin' and Slidin') alongside early songs such as 'It's Not My Fault' and the studio master 'Reminiscing' itself.

Whether the songs needed overdubbing or not, they all got it (except 'Reminiscing'), from a band Petty was working with – the Fireballs. To Petty, this was an opportunity to promote his protégés, as well as to make money out of the Buddy Holly catalogue. Although Jerry Allison would later complain that if Norman felt he needed drums on the session it would have made more musical sense to ask him to do it, Petty can't really be blamed for looking to the future as well as the past – an approach vindicated in his terms when the Fireballs, together with vocalist Jimmy Gilmer, had a huge US hit with 'Sugar Shack' later in 1963.

In the autumn of that year, the last Buddy Holly single to make the UK top ten, 'Wishing', was issued, and peaked exactly at number ten. Once again, it had detrimental overdubbing on what had been a perfectly satisfactory studio version of the song to start with. The logical choice for the next single would have been 'Love's Made A Fool Of You', not least since by now the existence of the track was well known and Holly fans were eager for it. Instead, they got a version of 'What To Do' which Petty had overdubbed with the Fireballs – a vast improvement on the Jack Hansen version, but not really a new song by any stretch of the imagination. Even so, it made number 27 on the UK chart. Fans had to wait until 1971 for the release of all the Norman Petty versions of the Apartment Tapes originals, on a good album, *Remember*, which included other rarities such as the original version of 'Maybe Baby'. The versions of the Apartment Tapes with the Fireballs on are far from perfect and suffer in particular from a heavy electric bass, where Buddy would surely have used stand-up bass. To me, some of the tracks, especially 'That's What They Say' and 'Learning The Game', actually sound, on the original undubbed tapes, as if Buddy intended them for string arrangements, like the last session at the Pythian Temple studio.

The mixture of Holly recordings from different times and different places, with and without over-dubbing, was repeated on the album *Showcase* in 1964. The mish-mash wasn't what Holly fans wanted – we wanted songs grouped together in the order they had been recorded, with as little interfer-ence as possible – but it was all we had. *Showcase* peaked at number three on the chart. More or less to coincide with the album, 'You've Got Love' was released as a single, but got only to number 40; in Australia, bizarrely, 'I'm Gonna Love You Too', the original B-side of 'Listen to Me', was released because another group, the Hullabaloos, had released a cover in a similar style to the original, and this Holly re-release reached number six. A UK re-issue of 'Peggy Sue' failed to chart, although it reached number 34 in Australia, and when 'Love's Made A Fool Of You' did eventually come out, almost exactly a year after 'Wishing', it crept only to number 39 in the UK chart. This was essentially the end of Buddy Holly's success on the singles chart.

With albums, though, it was a different story. 1965 brought the release of a collection of Buddy and Bob material, titled, with an indifference to the geography of the flat Texas plain so breathtaking that it can only be admired, *Holly in the Hills*. Even Buddy would surely have been amazed to see this collection of western-style country from the mid-1950s reach number thirteen on the UK album chart ten years after it was recorded; he would also surely have been appalled by the insensitive and heavy-handed over-dubbing, which included the addition of drums to real country music.

That might have been the end of the story, but the success of a greatest hits package in 1967 encouraged Norman Petty to go back to the well one more time and come up with the album *Giant*, released in the spring of 1969. The extent to which he was scraping the barrel is clear from the inclusion of insensitively overdubbed versions of 'You're The One' and 'Dearest', which had already appeared in much cleaner form on *Showcase*. Ironically, the songs Petty probably regarded least are the most interesting ones – 'Blue Monday', 'Ain't Got No Home', and 'Good Rockin' Tonight'. All suffer from the overdubbing, but underneath can be heard Buddy and J.I. having a ball. Like *Holly in the Hills*, *Giant* reached number thirteen in the UK album chart, ten years after Buddy Holly died and thirteen years after some of the songs on it were recorded. It seemed like the end. But the 1970s brought a dramatic revival of interest in Buddy Holly and his music (a revival in the US, that is; in the UK he'd never been forgotten) through a combination of circumstances.

The first catalyst was Don McLean's song 'American Pie', released late in 1971, with its reference to 'the day the music died'. The huge success of the song stimulated interest in the music McLean was singing about, and saw an upsurge in sales of Buddy Holly material, including several less-than-satisfactory compilation albums. Then along came Linda Ronstadt. After years struggling to make a mark in the music business, she made a breakthrough in 1974 with the album *Heart Like a Wheel*, which featured her version of 'It Doesn't Matter

Anymore'. Released as a single, this reached just number 47 on the Hot 100. But under the guiding influence of her producer Peter Asher, a Holly fan who had himself had a hit with 'True Love Ways' (with Gordon Waller in 1965), in 1976 she climbed to number eleven with 'That'll Be The Day', and in 1977 'It's So Easy' took her all the way to number five. The following year, the movie *The Buddy Holly Story* was released. It's an entertaining work of fiction, but not the place to look for the truth about Buddy's life. Ask Larry Holley: 'Forget about that movie completely. Put it completely out of your mind. That movie was entirely erroneous. We were very disappointed.' (*Memories*)

Some idea of the (in)accuracy of the movie can be gleaned from the appearance of mountains in the background in scenes supposedly set in Lubbock, and the fact that the 'Buddy Holly' character is playing models of guitar that were not manufactured until long after the real Buddy Holly had died. Jerry Allison was as scathing as Larry Holley about the movie. 'They spelled Buddy's name right,' he said, but that 'was about the only thing they had right.' (quoted by Amburn)

But at least the movie did bring Buddy Holly's music to the attention of a younger audience. A compilation under the title *20 Golden Greats* became his only UK number one album in 1978, the year the movie came out, and sold over a million copies. The best thing about the movie, though, was that it encouraged a lot of angry people to try to set the record straight. Sonny Curtis was moved to write and record a single, 'The Real Buddy Holly Story', which packs more truth into a little over three minutes than there is in the whole movie, and Paul McCartney borrowed the title from Sonny for a TV documentary (still available on DVD) that is still the best place to find out what really happened. And if you just want entertainment, but with a sound basis in fact, the musical *Buddy* seems destined to run forever.

In a review of *The Buddy Holly Story* for *Rolling Stone*, Dave Marsh put his finger on just why Buddy Holly was so important a musician:

> One of Buddy Holly's greatest contributions was his involvement with every step of the record making process: production, arranging, writing and, as one of the pioneers of the overdub, even engineering.
>
> In a way it's this part of Holly's vision that is his greatest legacy. Today [in 1978], rock musicians

are free to spend months in the studio trying to craft perfect recordings without much corporate interference, in large part because of battles fought by such earlier musicians. Holly helped to contribute to rock the notion that it was possible to do it all, no matter what anybody said.

Now, of course, with modern technology it's possible to do it all at home, without even using a studio, and to make the music available online immediately. How Buddy would have loved that!

Since the 1970s, as he has come to be regarded as a figure of historical importance, not merely a dead singer, compilations of Buddy Holly recordings have continued to appear, no longer with any interference from Norman Petty (who died in 1984) but still constrained by questions of who owns what rights. The quality of the presentation of this material has gradually improved, and it is now possible to get collections in some cases grouped by the year they were recorded, and often without intrusive overdubbing. If you include bootlegs, *everything* is available, somewhere.

What Holly fans really want, of course, is a complete collection in chronological order, with a full description of when and where each recording was made. It wouldn't be too difficult. There are only just over 100 Buddy Holly recordings – the exact number depends on which of the alternative versions and out-takes you include – and played in sequence they show (in less than four hours) the musical development of one of the most significant artists of the twentieth century. Because of both his importance and the relatively small amount of material, Buddy Holly is the prime candidate for the same kind of treatment that the Beatles got with their *Anthology* collection. Fifty years on, it would be a fitting finale.

But perhaps Buddy Holly already has an even more fitting epitaph. When he died, he didn't have an enemy in the world – if you don't count Norman Petty, and who would want to count him? As Sonny Curtis wrote in 'The Real Buddy Holly Story':

He never knocked nobody down in his life;
He loved us all, and he treated us right.

And that, when you come down to it, matters even more than the music.

Sources and Further Reading

The number of books about Buddy Holly is itself a sign of his enduring popularity. They are a mixed bunch, but all of them contain something for the dedicated fan. The definitive full-length biography for anyone unfamiliar with Buddy Holly is the one by Philip Norman, but John Goldrosen's collaboration with John Beecher is also a must-read, especially for people who already know the music. Ellis Amburn's book is the least reliable, according to people who knew Buddy, but I include it for completeness. Larry Holley's memoirs give the best insight into how hard life was for the Holley family when Buddy was a child. The one by Elizabeth and Ralph Peer is mostly pictures and music for 36 songs associated with Buddy. Dave Laing concentrates on an analysis of the music, and his book makes fascinating reading in spite of its age and a tendency to take Norman Petty's claims at face value. Alan Mann's *A–Z* is a mine of encyclopaedic information, while the book by Anne Bustard and Kurt Cyrus is very American and aimed at very young readers. Richard Peters' account is superficial, but contains some great pictures; much the same is true of John Tobler's contribution. Of the two books called *The*

Day the Music Died, the one by Martin Huxley and Quinton Skinner is a slim volume based on a VH1 TV programme, focusing on the events surrounding the crash and including material not screened on TV; quotes from this source are indicated in the text by the note 'VH1'. The book by Larry Lehmer is much more extensive, and a good place to find out more about Ritchie Valens and the Big Bopper. My aim is not to compete with any of these books, but to provide an introduction to the life of Buddy Holly in the context of his music, and some insight into the man behind the music. *They Died Too Young* is a tiny book (breast pocket size) containing a surprising amount of information, but not all of it correct.

Ellis Amburn, *Buddy Holly* (Virgin, London, 2002)

Anne Bustard and Kurt Cyrus, *Buddy* (Simon & Schuster, New York, 2005)

Alan Clark, *Buddy Holly and the Crickets* (Alan Clark Productions, West Covina, California, 1979)

Jim Dawson and Spencer Leigh, *Memories of Buddy Holly* (Big Nickel Publishing, Winter Haven, Florida, 1996)

Peggy Sue Gerron and Glenda Cameron, *Whatever Happened to Peggy Sue?* (TogiEntertainment, Oklahoma, 2008)

John Goldrosen, *The Buddy Holly Story* (Quick Fox, London, 1979). This book was updated in collaboration with John Beecher and reissued as *Remembering Buddy* (Omnibus Books/Rollercoaster, London, 1996)

Larry Holley, *The Buddy I Knew!* (Larry Holley, Lubbock, 1979)

Larry Holley, *I Don't Know How I Did It* (Larry Holley, Lubbock, 2007)

Martin Huxley and Quinton Skiller, *The Day the Music Died* (Pocket Books, New York, 2000)

Dave Laing, *Buddy Holly* (November Books/Studio Vista, London, 1971)

Larry Lehmer, *The Day the Music Died* (Schirmer Books, New York, 1997)

Alan Mann, *The A–Z of Buddy Holly* (Aurum, London, 1996)

Philip Norman, *Buddy: The Biography* (Macmillan, London, 1996)

Richard Peters, *The Legend that is Buddy Holly* (Souvenir, London, 1990)

Elizabeth and Ralph Peer, *Buddy Holly* (Peer International, New York, 1972)

Terry Pratchett, *Soul Music* (Gollancz, London, 1994)

Tom Stockdale, *They Died Too Young: Buddy Holly* (Parragon, Bristol, 1995)

John Tobler, *The Buddy Holly Story* (Plexus, London, 1979)

There are two good DVDs available: *The Real Buddy Holly Story* (White Star), produced and endorsed by long-time Holly fan Paul McCartney; and *The Definitive Story*, part of a package that includes a 'best of' music CD (Universal). The VH1 programme *Behind the Music: The Day the Music Died* is also worth viewing, but seems to be unavailable.

See also:

http://buddyhollyonline.com/
and:
http://www.buddyhollycenter.org/

There are several Buddy Holly clips available on YouTube. For Buddy Holly records, see:
http://www.rollercoasterrecords.com/

More information about Buddy Holly's recording sessions can be found at: http://buddyholly.user.fr

Index